Psalms for Worship

E M Blaiklock

Commentary on the Psalms

Volume 2

Psalms for Worship

Psalms 73-150

A. J. Holman Company
division J. B. Lippincott Company
Philadelphia and New York

The poem 'Prayer' by C. S. Lewis is from
POEMS by C. S. Lewis, edited by Walter Hooper,
© 1964 by the Executors of the Estate of
C. S. Lewis. Reprinted by permission of Harcourt
Brace Jovanovich, Inc, and Collins Publishers Ltd.

U.S. Library of Congress Cataloging in Publication Data

> Blaiklock, E M
>   Psalms in worship.
>
>   (His Commentary on the Psalms; v. 2)
>   1. Bible. O.T. Psalms LXXIII-CL—Commentaries.
>   I. Title.
>   BS1430.3.B53   vol. 2   223'.2'07s   [223'.2'07]   77-2875
>   ISBN-0-87981-081-5

Designed by Tony Cantale

Printed by Hazell Watson and Viney Ltd,
Aylesbury, Bucks, England

Publisher's Introduction

The book of Psalms surely needs little introduction to the Christian reader. The hymnbook of the Jewish Temple, has from the very first been an important part of the Christian heritage. The quality of their poetry, the majestic grandeur of their vision of the Creator-God, their perceptive insights into human nature and their simple piety have made them an indispensable part of both public worship and private devotion. Joy and sorrow, trust and doubt, success and failure, hope and despair – all human experience is reflected here and each of us can readily identify with the struggles and sentiments of the original writers. Their profound statements about man's relationship with God and with his fellows speak with a renewed potency and relevancy to every age. It is this that Professor Blaiklock helps us to see in these pages. Each Psalm is firmly placed in its original setting in an introductory paragraph, and verse by verse comments bring out the abiding relevance and contemporary significance.

These books have been designed primarily as a devotional commentary, but their content and layout will make them the ideal basis for a daily reading programme. Most Psalms are of a suitable length for this purpose and others will easily subdivide. Readers will probably find that the RSV is the most useful version but Professor Blaiklock has used a wide variety of translations, some of which are designated by the abbreviations listed below.

Abbreviations

AAT	An American Translation, Smith and Goodspeed
JB	Jerusalem Bible
KJV	Authorised (King James) Version
LB	The Living Bible
NASB	New American Standard Bible
NEB	New English Bible
RSV	Revised Standard Version
RV	English Revised Version
LXX	Septuagint (Greek Version of the Old Testament)

Author's Preface

The Psalter is a book of prayers rather than a prayer book. Its words leap to the page from the heart of man, racked by pain, jubilant with joy, despairing, aspiring, questioning, worshipping, but never ceasing to reach for God.

The world changes, knowledge grows, but the heart of man remains as it has always been. That is why the psalms become increasingly, as life goes on, the mirror and the language of experience, the book which speaks to us, and provides the words for the hours of contrition, of fear, of awe, defeat and victory.

And that is why each reader of the psalms could write his own commentary. This book is as the writer's life has made it. It is called a devotional commentary in the hope that, like the psalms themselves, it may add meaning to some reader's experience and sharpen the relevance of words already immortal.

The psalms are poetry and, like all poetry, have meaning which varies with the mood, the perplexity or the passion which each one who reads them brings to his reading. What strikes home to one may pass another by. When any commentator can comment on great poetry with cold detachment, he has lost the ability to comment. On the other hand a poem may mean to a reader more than the poet first intended. This perhaps is the test of true poetry, and especially of the poetry of the Bible, in which God's Spirit had a part.

Here, then, with what elucidation one man's mind and life's experience may bring, is a book about the psalms. The paths man treads are trodden well and their rough places and their plain are old familiar ground. A guide can sometimes help, and a guidebook, imperfect, no doubt, and certainly incomplete, is the book which follows.

E. M. Blaiklock

Titirangi
Auckland N.Z.

73

Read Psalm 73; Jeremiah 1; Malachi 3.14–18

Occasion and author

A psalm of Asaph appeared in Book 2, along with some psalms of Korah. Book 3 contains many psalms of Asaph along with a psalm of David, a psalm by one Ethan and some songs of Korah. It appears from the historical books that Asaph was a temple music-master who did much to beautify the services with song (1 Chron. 15.17,19; 25.1; 2 Chron. 29.30). It is possible that he made an original collection of psalms which was later partially broken up on considerations of subject matter by the final editor or compiler. The psalms of Asaph need not have been composed completely by him. The works of Homer in the ancient Greek collection contain hymns not necessarily by that great but shadowy poet. Even the corpus of Shakespeare is invaded by Beaumont and Fletcher. This is of no consequence. The work and authority of Asaph's poetic and spiritual contribution to the Psalter was rightly recognized by the rabbis.

The theme of this fine poem is as old as thinking man. It appeared in Psa. 37. It is the theme of Habakkuk and the Book of Job. The Hebrew mind found rest and truth in the concept of one just and almighty God, who therefore was bound to reward the good and punish the wicked. But experience challenged that belief. Especially in the days of the great invasions and the captivities, it was obvious that the good suffered with the bad, and unmerited agony fell on the upright and the pure. Even in private life it was too often evident that evil prospered and good went unrewarded. Psa. 37 finds its Old Testament solution in patience. 'Wait and you will see', and in human life it is true that the end of the wicked is often a demonstration of ultimate punishment. Job reaches a conclusion in the light of all that was in his day revealed about the ways of God, which would leave the modern mind in despair. 'Who are you,' says God in the whirlwind, 'to question what I decree?' It is true that 'the ways of God are past finding out', that the wisdom of the Lord transcends that of man as the heavens are higher than the earth, but the tormented soul asks for a far greater assurance than Job found. Jeremiah, in his first chapter, observing the scalding brew of terror pouring over the land, was also shown the vision of 'the wakeful tree', the almond, a sign of assurance that God knew, and that history was not out of control. Habakkuk, faced with the utter helplessness of the little land before the invasion of Nebuchadnezzar, was told simply to believe. Faith would ultimately be vindicated. Malachi (3.14–18) found a solution to despair in the same faith and a glimpse of immortality and a righting of all wrong in a

9

wider context. Psa. 73 is much like this. When the writer was driven to his poem of pain and faith cannot be guessed.

Commentary

1 The storm is over. 'The elements sweetly rest.' The writer has had an encounter with doubt, as the faithful do, and has come from the struggle triumphant. Doubt is a common experience but cannot be a way of life. Unbelief does not doubt. It is faith that doubts. 'He who has never had a doubt', wrote Archbishop Whateley in 1847, 'who believes what he believes for reasons which he thinks as irrefragable (if that is possible) as a mathematical demonstration, ought not to be said so much to *believe* as to *know* . . . It is rather he who believes – not indeed without the exercise of his reason, but with knowledge and appreciation of formidable objections, it is this man who may most truly be said intelligently to believe.' Dr. J. J. S. Perowne quotes Bishop Hind's poem:

> *Yet so it is; belief springs still*
> *In souls that nurture doubt;*
> *And we must go to him who will*
> *The baneful weed cast out.*
>
> *Did ever thorns thy path beset?*
> *Beware – be not deceived;*
> *He who has never doubted yet*
> *Has never yet believed.*

2 The story of the grim experience of doubt begins. The ground on which faith stood became slippery beneath the feet. It is disillusionment bitter and complete when all the standards by which a man has lived seem suddenly proved invalid, and evil bears the benediction that he had thought belonged only to good.

3 It was an awful moment when he, an unrewarded follower of God, found his mind tempted to wish he were like the arrogant and to envy the immunity of the wicked. As the Jerusalem Bible renders it, he discovered himself 'envying the arrogant . . . and watching the wicked get rich.'

4 'Bands' (KJV) is an odd word. 'Pangs' (RSV) is probably the correct rendering of the hidden metaphor, the sharp constricting pain, the fettering agony of the body's breakdown is suggested. Through sick eyes he had watched the wicked. To all appearances they seemed to live well and to die without suffering.

5 'No part have they in human cares,' Moffatt renders, 'no blows like other men.' Like the disillusioned of Malachi's third chapter, the tormented man seemed to see what he had not dared to look upon before, the actual preservation of the wicked. They appeared to have chosen the better part.

6 And they realize it for 'they flaunt their pride like a necklace, violence wraps them like clothing' (R. K. Harrison). Clothes cover, protect, envelop, preserve, like 'the grace which covers all my sin'. Is it not a fact of experience that the clothing of a person is the first impression his presence makes? Before a word of speech has revealed a personality, the outward appearance has confronted the sight. Violence was the first impression these contemporaries made on the embittered psalmist in the trough of his pain.

7 They come closer, and the face is seen, bloated with their greed, 'vice oozing from their soul', as Moffatt vigorously continues. Such folk have always lived ... 'the face of the stuffed swine', as Masefield saw in the city street.

8 And no furtive wickedness is theirs. This makes it harder to bear. They spoke openly, challenging the judgement of God. Mussolini once demonstrated the folly of fearing God, to his own satisfaction. He placed his watch on the table and gave the Almighty five minutes in which to strike him dead. The garage in Milan with the bloated corpse hanging by the feet was forty years away.

9 God permits such tongues to 'strut through the earth' (RSV).

10 'For this reason,' Harrison renders, 'people resort to them, and greedily gulp down their pronouncements.' The packed Piazza Venezia, roaring 'Duce, Duce', as the plump figure with out-thrust chin stood on the Palazzo balcony ... The Hebrew is difficult. 'The fullness of water is drained by them', the words run literally. Surely the deluded people are in view, gulping thirstily what they desire to hear. RSV's 'and find no fault in them' is weak.

11 It all feeds the arrogance of those who thus seduce and deceive. Or is it not rather those who are seduced and deceived who are led to the deadliest damage, as the psalmist was in the hour of his doubt? 'God cannot care. Can He even know?' Chilling thought.

12 There then you have them, he ends bitterly. Here is the highway to success. Cast God aside and you will prosper.

13,14 ''Tis all in vain I kept my heart from stain, kept my life clean, when all day long blows fell on me, and every dawn brought some chastening!' So Moffatt on this Job-like passage. Justice was awry. Pain and privation fell on the undeserving good. The bad prospered.

15 God's hand at this point seems to have been laid on his hot heart. He could not say words like these, though now he is free to record the strength of the temptation. The words in the heart are the better for being words on paper, when they become thus part of the story of a battle and a victory.

16,17 'I set myself to read the riddle,' Knox translates, 'but it proved a hard search, until I betook myself to God's sanctuary, and considered, there, what becomes of such men at last.' In the Temple (cf. 1 Sam. 1.13ff. and Luke 18.10ff.) illumination came to the psalmist as it came to Isaiah (6.1–7). Habakkuk had his 'watchtower' whither he retired to examine in prayer the awful problem of human pain and God's strange tolerance of Babylon's sin. Abraham had some 'place where he stood before the Lord'. The 'sanctuary' may be in many places, but in the psalmist's case it was probably the shrine in Jerusalem.

18 The answer broke suddenly upon him. It was not he, but they, who stood on a slippery slope. Is this merely the conclusion of 37.9–11, demonstrably though not universally true – at least to outward appearance? In v. 4 he has admitted that they die in their beds, these blasphemers, too often for justice. But if God be just, justice must somewhere be done, even if it is not seen to be done. The first step to understanding is, therefore, to take the whole of life into account.

19 Does this sudden asseveration indicate an illuminating insight into what is undoubtedly a lifelong punishment on evil – the lack of what the godly stores in the treasury of the heart? It is a fact that the godless lack most of that which makes life worth living, a peace in the heart, a consuming purpose, hope, confidence in a divine plan, a victory over death, 'some late lark singing', and a multitude of by-products of such stability in health, home, mind . . . The mind committed to evil, the darkened heart, lacks vital constituents of happiness, and never knows what it has missed. But even this falls short of retribution unless there is what Aristotle called, in his analysis of Greek tragedy, 'the Recognition' – the piercing, late understanding of folly, sin and loss when it is all past remedy. That is why this psalm does not grasp the full solution – there is a Great White Throne.

20   In this verse the psalmist almost breaks through to such final understanding. He sees at least the transience of the flaunted prosperity which has stirred his ire and roused his doubts. He sees the whole sorry puppet show of evil's apparent triumph momentarily through God's eyes. MacLaren puts it well. 'It is obvious,' he writes, 'that there are many other considerations which have to be taken into account in order to find a complete solution of the problem of this psalm. But the psalmist's solution goes a long way to lighten the painful perplexity of it', and if we add his succeeding thoughts as to the elements of true blessedness, we have solution enough for peaceful acquiescence, if not for entire understanding. The psalmist's way of finding an answer is even more valuable than the answer which he found. They who dwell in 'the secret place of the Most High' can look upon the riddle of this painful world with equanimity, and be content to leave it half unsolved.

21,22   In the place and hour of revelation he also saw himself. How foolish he had been, how brutish in his understanding, thus to question God. He stands for a moment where Job stood and abhors himself . . .

23   But only for a moment. His God is less magisterial and more paternal than the God who spoke out of the whirlwind to Job. Like Christ grasping Peter's hand when he was 'beginning to sink', God has laid hold of the suppliant's. Harrison renders: 'Nevertheless I am always in Your presence. You have grasped me by my right hand.'

24,25   And along this path, that of an Eternal Presence, some glimmering of faith in another life seems to break through. The verb 'take' is that used of Enoch (Gen. 5.24) and of Elijah's translation (2 Kings 2.3,5,9,10). Luther had a luminous rendering: 'If I only hold fast to Thee, Heaven and earth are a matter of no concern' (Wenn ich nur dich habe, so frage ich nichts nach Himmel und Eide).

26   'Though heart and body fail, yet God is my possession for ever' (NEB). One could wish that the psalm had pursued this growing enlightenment further. The psalmist seems verse by verse to move nearer to the Christian's solution.

27,28   He now sees those who stirred his passion so as the poor ephemeral things they were, and his own utter blessedness in God.

Conclusion
Let it be MacLaren's: '. . . the psalmist has gathered up the double truth . . . To be absent from God is to perish. Distance from him is separation from life. Drawing near to him is the only good . . . By the effort of his own volition he has made God his refuge, and, safe in him, he can bear the sorrow of the godly, and look unenvying on the prosperity of sinners . . .'

Read Psalm 74; Lamentations 1

Occasions and author

This is a psalm of Asaph, but obviously not from the pen of the historical Asaph of David's day. The criteria elude us but clearly the Asaph psalm was a composition in a certain style and tradition recognizable to those who put the collection together.

This is a lament in the style of Jeremiah's own Lamentations. The city is desolate, its defences down, its sanctuary defiled, the land ravaged, while God appeared not to care. There is no reason to suppose that the psalm was as late as the times of the Maccabees when Antiochus Epiphanes thus looted, defiled and destroyed city and people (165–168 B.C.) It was undoubtedly a time when the heavens were silent and no prophetic voice was heard (9). The objection is that the Psalter probably attained its final form before so late a date.

Other dates appear more likely. Esarhaddon made one of Assyria's destructive forays into Palestine at a time quite notably barren in prophetic leadership (2 Chron. 33.11), but the utter desolation of this psalm demands more than this time of sorrow. It is more likely a psalm of the Exile, referring to Nebuchadnezzar's destruction of Jerusalem. Nor need it be dated a generation later when Jeremiah and Ezekiel were dead. We have no means of assessing the standing of either prophet among the exiles. Indeed, the Lachish letters and Jeremiah's own historical chapters suggest that he was not popular, and neither prophet was necessarily commonly known.

Laments were a common form of literature, a universal catharsis of grief. The *threnoi* of Greek poetry and the dirges of Scotland are in the same tradition. When Wroxeter, last shred of Roman Britain, fell in A.D. 582, the poet Llyarc Hen wrote the death song of Uriconium, 'the White City in the valley' of Kyndylan last of the Roman-British rulers. It was forsaken 'without fire, without light, without song', its silence broken only by the scream of the eagle 'who has drunk the heart's blood of Kyndylan the fair'. It is natural that men should be moved by such destruction, and it is a mark against the humanity of modern man that the century's vast ruins, from Stalingrad to Hiroshima, stir no song, no poetry and small pity. For the psalmist there was more than pity at the murder of the works of men. There was immense and awful perplexity. 'Why, O God, why?'

Commentary

1,2 'The sheep of thy pasture', is a phrase common in the psalms of the Exile (79.13; 95.7; 100.3). The poet in his agony sees his people as helpless, bewildered creatures, not the deserving sufferers of enormous and irreparable disaster. 'Why are You forever rejecting us, Lord? Why does Your anger fume against Your grazing flock?' (Harrison). And helplessly he reminds the God of history of His part in assembling the flock.

3,4 Psa. 79, which seems to refer to the same event, speaks of death in the streets. This poem thinks chiefly of the blasphemous ruin inflicted with impunity upon the lovely shrine. The cold account of Nebuchadnezzar refers to the capture of Jerusalem. 'In the seventh year, in the month of Kislev, the Babylonian King mustered his troops, and having marched to the land of Hatti, besieged the city of Judah, and on the second day of the month of Adar took the city . . .' March 16, 597 B.C. is the date. The psalmist reveals the agony from the other side. Even the pagan standards and ensigns were placed there.

5–7 Like woodmen felling a forest they attacked the lovely woodwork. 'They smashed the doors down with their axes, like woodmen felling trees' (5, Moffatt). 'They ripped the carvings clean out, they smashed them with hatchet and pick' (6, NEB).

8 There were no synagogues, if the early date of this psalm is to stand, and Jerusalem had the one unrivalled shrine. In every town, however, there could well have been without offence some place of assembly, some ancestor of the synagogue. It is a method of oppression to destroy all memorials and symbols of the past. Hadrian made a clean sweep of the synagogues of the land after the Bar-Kochbar rebellion in A.D. 132, 133 and the Babylonians, in the name of Marduk, may well have done as much to Israel.

9 And no voice of insight and authority could suggest the reason why. 'We no longer see our symbols, and there is no one among us who knows how long it will last.' (Harrison)

10,11 If God would only act, instead of standing like a man unconcerned, His idle hand thrust into the fold of His robe.

12–15 He once worked obviously on earth (12), tore the opposing sea apart (13), drowning the Egyptians (the 'crocodiles', 'dragons'), destroying the Leviathan, mighty Egypt (14). He burst the rock to give drink to the thirsty ('cleave the fountain' (KJV) is a proleptic expression – 'cleave the rock so as to make a fountain.') And He divided Jordan (15).

16,17 The alternations of light and darkness, the parade of the ordered seasons, all suggest that He who once lived still lives. Nothing else is changed, only the visible hand of intervention, protection and rescue.

18–23 Hence the passionate plea for justice and salvation. The gentle ('thy dove') are handed over to wild beasts. Even the refugees, crowding every cave and hole in the land (20), have been hunted down and savagely mistreated. And God once promised, made a 'covenant'. It could not be annulled. The psalm becomes excruciating in its communication of agony. 'The oppressed, the poor, the needy' were put to shame and horror under the boots of cruelty (21), and God's own good name was at stake. 'When wilt Thou save the people, Oh, God of Mercy, when?' . . . 'Reverent earnestness of supplication,' MacLaren comments, 'sometimes sounds like irreverence, but "when the heart's deeps boil in earnest", God understands the meaning of what sounds strange, and recognizes the profound trust in His faithfulness and love which underlies bold words.'

Conclusion

The psalm ends without relief. It is harrowing to read. Life sometimes calls forth such supplication, and God's delay or apparent inaction is agony to bear. Other psalms show a breaking through to faith and a quietening of the heart. Not this. The passion of the prayer never diminishes. We see more deeply into the heart of the Exile than anywhere else.

75,76

Read Psalms 75; 76

Occasion and author

Another Asaph composition is found here and there is nothing further to add to that ascription. Such psalms are invariably of a high artistic merit, a lofty spirituality, and commonly of a national and collective rather than an individual character.

The occasion might again be the jubilant months which followed the disaster to Sennacherib's invasion when Judah passed through an experience of relief perhaps matched in Elizabethan England after the breaking of the Armada. It is possible that the psalm was written a score of years later than the invasion, when Sennacherib himself fell under the swords of his own sons, while he was worshipping in the temple of Nisroch (2 Kings 19.37). That was in 681 B.C. and the assassination in the savage empire, for all the likelihood that the murdered man's successor would be another as evil, may have taken some portion of uneasiness from the menaced neighbours of the Assyrians.

Commentary

75.1 The reading and translation of the RV and the NEB give good sense. 'Thy name is brought very near to us in the story of thy wonderful deeds' (NEB). Perhaps the sense is: 'Thy name springs readily to our mind or lips'. Compare Deut. 4.7: 'What nation is there that has God so near to them?'

2 God is made abruptly to intervene: 'When the time is ripe, I will judge in fairness' (Harrison). 'The congregation' is a meaning of the word used, but quite inappropriate here. The word (*mo'ed*) means an appointed time or place, and by extension those assembled. It was singularly obtuse of the KJV to render in the last sense.

3 The sum of things seems about to crumble but God reminds those who listen that He holds the supports.

4 The moral law, too, still stands, which judges ultimately the arrogant and the flaunters of transient power.

5 The uplifted horn and the stiffened neck are the signs and symbols of arrogance, aggression and pride. Of such sort had been Sennacherib. 'Do not flaunt your power, nor speak with wanton presumption' (Harrison). Sennacherib's inscriptions about the campaign of 701 B.C. are a perfect illustration of such sanguinary and mindless boasting: '. . . I drew near to Ekron, and slew the governors and nobles who had rebelled and hung their bodies on stakes round the city . . . As for Hezekiah the Jew, who did not bow to my yoke, forty-six of his fortresses I stormed and took. Two hundred thousand people . . . I brought away captive . . . Hezekiah, like a caged bird, I shut up in Jerusalem, his royal city. Anyone coming out of the city gate I turned back to his misery . . .' An age used to the bombast and false-hoods of tyrants' propaganda, can recognize the confession of a siege which failed. Sennacherib's boasts cover the campaign at length. If the psalm is dated 681 B.C., the psalmist's words are barbed comment.

6 'No power from the east nor from the west, no power from the wilderness, can raise a man up' (NEB). 'Promotion' of the KJV is an unhappy word. The psalm was not in the hands of a felicitous translator. (It is a curious fact that those who can speak with such confidence of stylistic variety in remote and difficult languages, never seem to have attempted a linguistic analysis of the translators of 1611.)

7 At any rate, here is the answer. 'No, God is Judge. He puts one down and lifts up another.'

8 In a vivid change of figure God is pictured holding the foaming cup of His judgement to the lips of the wicked, and making them swallow its last bitter dregs.

9,10 The psalmist concludes with a shout of jubilation, curiously identify-ing himself with the hand of God.

The succeeding psalm points with irresistible clarity to the same occasion of deliverance. Sennacherib's defeat at other hands than those of man stirred the religious fervour of the nation in a most notable fashion. Pss. 46–48 have already been discussed. This fine hymn extends the list.

76.1 The mention of Israel along with Judah may allude to the fact that Hezekiah was the first ruler of the southern kingdom to attempt a reunion of Judah and Israel. After the tragic fall of Samaria and the devastation of the northern kingdom by Sargon in 721 there was little left for salvage. We do, however, read that Hezekiah sent to 'all Israel and Judah and also to Ephraim and Manasseh, that they should come to the house of the Lord in Jerusalem to keep the Passover for the Lord God of Israel' (2 Chron. 30.1). The words may be a slender foundation on which to build, but it does seem clear that Hezekiah, inspired, perhaps, by Isaiah's global vision, made some attempt to recover the loss of the northern kingdom. Had others followed his missionary lead perhaps the problems of John 4, the rift between Samaritan and Jew, might not have arisen. This is a better explanation of the opening verse, than to ascribe its form merely to the parallelism which was the common form of Hebrew poetry.

2 This granted, it is also true, as the Lord told the Samaritan woman, that Jerusalem was the Holy City, symbolic of all God meant to the Hebrew people.

3 In fact the disaster which fell on the Assyrian host took place far to the south, but God, established beyond space, place and time could be said to act in, or from, the place of His abiding – Zion or Salem (Jerusalem).

4 A difficult verse. There seems a reminiscence of Isa. 14.25. 'I will break the Assyrian in my land, and upon my mountains trample him underfoot.' 'The mountains of prey' (KJV and several other versions) is difficult to interpret. It could mean, interpreting the Hebrew prefix thus translated 'than', as rather a literal expression of 'direction from': 'Glorious art Thou and lordly, descending from the mountains of prey' – that is, from the hill-country where the disaster to the foe occurred. RSV follows the LXX – 'Glorious art thou, more majestic than the everlasting mountains'.

5 'They have sunk into their sleep' the verse concludes (2 Kings 19.35). The mighty men 'could not move a finger' (Moffatt).

The Assyrians are represented in their sculptures as men of crude muscular strength. They bend great bows, powerful enough to drive an arrow through the spine of a lion. And now, swept by the breath of Death's Angel, as Byron's poem had it, the great warriors were limp on the polluted earth, strength gone, hands lax.

6 Byron had the verse in mind:

> *And there lay the steed with his nostril all wide,*
> *But through it there rolled not the breath of his pride;*
> *And the foam of his gasping lay white on the turf,*
> *And cold as the spray of the rock-beaten surf.*
> *And there lay the rider, distorted and pale,*
> *With the dew on his brow and the rust on his mail.*

7–9 God as Judge is a common thought in the Asaph psalms. These verses resume the thread of thought in the previous psalm. Nature itself grew still. 'The earth was hushed in terror when thy sentence fell from heaven, when God arose to act on earth, in succour of the afflicted' (8,9, Moffatt). 'Even so come, Lord.'

10 The Jerusalem Bible may interpret this difficult verse: 'Man's wrath only adds to your glory. The survivors of your wrath you will draw like a girdle around you.' In other words all the raging of men shall appear so pathetically futile that God will, in the face of its feebleness, be magnified.

11,12 The conclusion points the lesson. MacLaren puts it well in his leisurely musing: 'Therefore men are summoned to vow and pay their vows. And while Israel is called to worship, the nations round about, who have seen the field of the dead, are called to do homage and bring tribute to Him who, as it so solemnly shows, can cut off the breath of the highest, or can cut down their pride, as the grape-gatherer does the cluster (for such is the allusion in the word 'cut down'). The last clause of the psalm, which stands somewhat disconnected from the preceding, gathers up the lessons of the tremendous event which inspired it, when it sets Him forth as to be feared by the kings of the earth.'

Occasion and author

The writer of this Asaph psalm is unknown. The occasion, as with many a psalm of David, is an experience of deep personal sorrow. Any sensitive reading of the psalm surely enforces this conclusion. The dwelling upon the hand of God in the nation's history is no indication that this was a national hymn from the days of the exile, when the deliverance from the earlier bondage and the crossing of the Red Sea was often in the minds of the dispossessed. Habakkuk 3.10–15 seems to be based upon this psalm, and, since Habakkuk wrote under the shadow of the coming Babylonian invasion, this would indicate an earlier date for the psalm – perhaps in Josiah's day. Admittedly, it would not be impossible to argue from the reverse direction, and maintain that the psalmist, an exiled sufferer, quoted Habakkuk. The impossibility of dogmatism in such areas of conjecture has been admitted.

Commentary

1 'My voice to God', is all that the psalmist says. One might write: 'My voice . . . to God', as though the gasp of his petition, and the divine name were all he could, in the pain of the moment, utter.

2 This is a terribly intense verse. The mute and voiceless holding out of suppliant hands in the darkness is deeply pathetic. Bishop Cecil Wilson of the Melanesian Mission at the turn of the century told how he lay in the dark in a dank hut in a Solomon Islands jungle. An attack of malaria seized him. 'As I lay on my bed and shivered,' he writes, 'the thought of Peter's wife's mother lying sick of a fever and the Lord taking her hand, and how the fever left her, came into my mind . . . I imagined His hand in mine . . . and the fever died away . . .' RSV puts the verse: '. . . in the night my hand is stretched out without wearying'.

> *There are times so dark that I cannot see*
> *Through the mist of His wise design,*
> *But though darkness hide, He is by my side*
> *With a touch of His hand on mine.*

3,4 God provides the words when the mind is too numb and the spirit too overwhelmed to find any – Paul's 'groanings which cannot be uttered' (Rom. 8.26).

5,6 The mind turns desperately to the past and seeks the vanished sunshine. 'I think over former days, I recall years long past' (Harrison).

7–9 And the grapple in the darkness continues with the whispering of doubt. 'Perhaps God has changed, no longer cares. Perhaps anger has closed the gates of His mercy.'

10 The doubt crystallizes. Here is sorrow to crown all sorrow. Worse than all other misery is the sudden fear that God indeed has changed and cares no more.

11 The remedy again is what has been noted before 'His love in times past forbids us to think . . .'

12 One must resolutely seek for meaning in the tangle and puzzle of events.

13–15 After all He cannot betray Himself and be less than holy.

16–20 This is a vivid and poetic picture of the great event of deliverance. It is not impossible that the vivid picture of storm and earthquake contains a tradition of a tempestuous night of wind and seismic disturbance which preceded the crossing of the Red Sea – and indeed provides some insight into the machinery of the miracle by which the waters were driven back to form a wall, that is, a defence (78.13), while the host crossed the denuded mudflats. The strong wind is mentioned in Exodus (14.21). The psalm completes the picture.

Conclusion

Let it be in the words of Bishop Perowne: 'So ends the Psalm. Nor can I see in such a close that abruptness which has led some commentators to suppose that the Psalm was never finished. The one great example is given and that is enough. All is included in that; and the troubled, desponding spirit has found peace and rest in the view of God's redemption . . .'

Read Psalm 78

Occasion and author

This historical psalm, a 'parable', as the writer calls it (2), rises to a climax with the establishment of David as king. It is a moral history of the Hebrew people ('I am going to speak to you in parable and expound the mysteries of our past', 2, JB). It seems probable therefore, that the psalm was written at the time of David's establishment as monarch of a united Israel. The references to Ephraim (9,67) might suggest some disaffection in that powerful northern tribe against the hegemony of Judah. The reference to a battlefield betrayal of a force of Ephraimite archers may be literal, unrecorded though such an event is. Commentators arbitrarily insist that it is a figure for spiritual defection. If such a date for the psalm is accepted, it follows that it could have been a poem from the pen of the original Asaph, the person who lived and wrote in David's day (1 Chron. 25.1, 2 Chron. 29.30). Perhaps it was written in Jerusalem (54 – ' . . .to yon mountain which His right hand had purchased', as Perowne renders it – literally 'this mountain', as though Zion was in full view). The location of the psalm at this point in the Psalter may have been suggested by the final strophe of the preceding psalm.

Commentary

1–72 The psalm is a unity, divisible into verses but not into strophes or sections. It must be viewed and read as a whole, for its force and impact are in its totality. It contains vivid snatches of description – the heaped tide of the waters under the steady blast of the wind (13), the migratory quail dropping exhausted into the camp (27,28). The flare of Philistine invasion (61–64) . . . A theme of mercy meeting ingratitude, of care and of judgement runs through the whole prophetic poem, and it should be read in three ways – in its original form as a national poem, with a shift of historical position as a description of the Church, stumbling through what Bunyan called, 'the desert of this world', and as a poem applicable to any one of us.

The Hebrew prophets saw history in the light of the moral law. Long before Herodotus, the 'Father of History', sought a meaning in a series of great events which had befallen Greece, two and a half millennia before A. J. Toynbee's ponderings, in his monumental *Study of History*, disengaged from the records of man those moral and spiritual principles which determine the rise and fall of nations, the thinkers and prophets of the Hebrews, in their musings on history, took for granted that the ways of man, his faith or his rebellion, his good and evil, determined the patterns of history, that there was a law at work which, accepted or scorned, accounted for the emergence and eclipse of peoples.

The final verse in the KJV is one of those renderings which might well be left to stand in subsequent translations, one of those turns of felicitous and lucid phrase which can hardly find improvement. It refers, of course, to one taken from the flocks to shepherd a people, but in the third reading of the psalm it might well be taken of the Shepherd of our souls. The Hebrew for hand in this beautiful verse is *caph*. Caph is the name of a letter in the Hebrew alphabet which is like a reversed capital C. The letter illustrates the meaning of the word. *Caph* is a hand ready to hold, quick to grasp, the hand from which no one snatches. *Caph* is not the hand ready to thrust or smite. There is another word for that. It is the hand which shapes, creates, forms things beautiful and good. The hand is useless save for aggression, unless the fingers bend. Such, in the psalm, was the hand of the careful Shepherd King. Such is the hand of God. God's guidance is the work of an inventive God, of a God who holds, shapes, plans.

79

Read Psalm 79; reread Psalm 74

Occasion and author

This psalm, of unknown authorship, tells of the catastrophe which inspired the earlier lament of Psa. 74. The occasion, it was there suggested, is much more likely to have been the destruction of Jerusalem by the Babylonian tyrant, Nebuchadnezzar, than the disasters of Antiochus Epiphanes' invasion. It is difficult to say whether the same poet wrote both laments. Similarities of language may be noticed, but there are also differences, and at such a distance in time, and in a language so remote, only the hardier literary critics would risk dogmatism. Jeremiah quoted vs. 6,7 (10.25) immediately after a quotation from Psa. 6. It can scarcely be doubted that Jeremiah was quoting the psalmist and not the psalmist the prophet. This need cause no difficulty over the dating. In the chapter containing the quotation, Jeremiah, to be sure, predicts the Captivity, but Jeremiah lived into the Captivity, and no one knows when he gave the chapter its final form. Such details are of no great significance. The theme is clear and sombre. The earlier lament bewailed the destruction of the temple. This speaks of the destruction of Judah, the abandoned dead and the bloodstained streets, a scene hideously familiar to the world of this murderous century.

Commentary

1 Pompey, the Roman General, entered the Holy of Holies in 66 B.C. So had the Babylonians earlier. Such defilement horrified the Jew. Perhaps those who are 'the temples of the Holy Spirit', might with profit catch a little of that ingrained revulsion. Godless feet can tread in more sanctuaries than one. Jerusalem itself was ruin, as Micah (3.12), speaking in Hezekiah's day, had foretold. Jeremiah, closer to the grim event, quoted the prophecy (26.18).

2,3 The ghastly picture of neglected dead among the broken ruins of their homes, has haunted history from Jerusalem to Hiroshima. It wrings the heart to think that man cannot have done with his devilry.

4 And what hurt the Jew was that he had boasted of his God, and now, beaten down in ash and dust and blood, he was a derision and a thing of ridicule, to be insulted, mocked and taunted for his faith.

5 The wondrous faith that, even under the burden of such heathen scorn, persists in believing that God has allowed disaster so dire, to punish, chastise, teach or to fulfil some other ultimately beneficent purpose, takes us to the very suffering heart of the Old Testament religion. God is never repudiated, even when addressed in hot and passionate words.

6,7 Surely if justice is anywhere enthroned in the bent and distorted scheme of things, God must punish, must unleash a righteous wrath on the men of blood who had done such evil to those who owned His name. 'They have destroyed your people Israel, invading every home.' There is agonizing pathos in the last words.

8,9 And as surely God must remember His afflicted people. Purge, chastise, cleanse, yes, let Him do all of this, but comes a time when faith staggers at the fierce contradiction, the bad uplifted, and the good trodden into a mire of blood and death. What of God's name, in a world so upside down? 'Haste in mercy to our side' (8, Knox) . . . 'for your name's sake'. The meaning is, as we have seen, 'because You are what You are'.

10 The train of thought may be traced through Joel (2.17) back to Exod. 32.12; Num. 14.15,16; Deut. 9.28.

11 This surely places the psalm in the time of the Captivity when 'the sons of death', as the Hebrew literally says, live in a strange land with no escape save through the grave.

12 The commination again intrudes, jarring to Christian ears. No one has licence to condemn who has not known the bitterness of the situation which wrings such a cry for vindication from the heart. These are the words of a soul almost maddened by overwhelming misery. They are part of Scripture in the same way as Jacob's lie to Esau is part of the Bible record. It is the will of God that the words stand thus to teach those who read what anguish can do to the spirit of man.

13 The quiet ending comes like a sob of relief. It leaves nothing more to be said.

Read Psalm 80

Occasion and author

Perhaps Calvin was correct in regarding this national hymn as a prayer of a southerner for the ruined northern kingdom. A heading in the Septuagint, which could retain an ancient tradition, refers the poem to the Assyrian invasion. The words of the recurrent refrain, which divides the psalm into strophes, suggest that those for whom it was written were in exile. The first person pronoun in these repeated appeals suggests, against Calvin's view, that the writer was one of those for whom he prays.

Commentary

1–3 Ephraim and Manasseh (2) are the two sons of Joseph (1), and their grouping has reference to the position the three tribes held behind the Ark

23

(Num. 2.17–24) in the desert march. The ancient shepherd walked ahead of his sheep, and the psalmist is picturing the desert march with God, invisible but real above the cherubim. 'Shine forth . . . stir up thy might,' he cries,and the reference to the ordered march surely implies a prayer that restoration will bring Ephraim and Manasseh, the sons of Joseph, and tribes of the afflicted north, back to the side of Benjamin, Rachel's other son and Joseph's brother. Benjamin had remained with Judah when the land was tragically divided. The prayer is, therefore, for unity. The reference to the old priestly benediction (Num. 6.25,26) completes the picture for any Israelite. He sees the host marching of old, God's presence a gleam above and before them.

4–7 The RSV is correct: 'Thou dost make us the scorn of our neighbours' (6). By this is meant not the great empires, but the border princedoms, always ready to enjoy the pain of Israel. God's chastisement, and the Psalmist never ceases to regard calamity as sent by God for His inscrutable purpose, was harder to bear because it fed the hate along the borderlands, and seemed to dishonour a God who was powerless to save those who trusted in Him.

8–15 Israel as the vine is a common figure (Isa. 5.1–7; 27.2–6; Jer. 2.21; 12.10; Ezek. 17.5–10). Hence five parables of Christ (Matt. 20.1–16; 21.28–32; Luke 20.9–18 especially). This fine sustained image of the vine tenderly transplanted, and sending its wide and fruitful shade across the land from Gaza to the Euphrates, only to have the frontiers of its fertility trampled by hogs and other beasts, while the husbandman, to all appearance, forgets what he has planted, is a fine piece of literature, as well as a vivid allegory, bitterly true to what had taken place.

16–19 The imagery continues. The last two clauses of v. 17 answer to the last two clauses of v. 15. The vine becomes a living, feeling, human creature, no mere insensitive plant of roots and stem and branches. It is a man whom God has planted, a nation set in the chosen soil of history, a being which feels, agonizes, thinks, and fails to understand.

Conclusion

This is precisely the point of pain. Why does God, who is Love, build all with love and then appear not to foster that on which He spent His love? Even pagan Omar makes his articulate pots surmise:

> *Then said another : 'Surely not in vain*
> *My Substance from the common Earth was ta'en,*
> *That He who subtly wrought me into Shape*
> *Should stamp me back to common Earth again.'*

> *Another said : 'Why, ne'er a peevish Boy*
> *Would break the Bowl from which he drank in Joy;*
> *Shall He that made the Vessel in pure Love*
> *And Fancy, in an after Rage destroy?'*

The psalmist faces the question as Habakkuk does, and finds the answer in faith. There is an ultimate chapter, a final page to turn and the answer is there in the words of a living God. God does not make to destroy, unless that which He made, being in His image, free-willed, at liberty to choose, as no vessel, no vine can be, deliberately chooses, promotes, and shapes his own destruction.

Read Psalm 81

Occasion and author

This hymn was probably written by some Levitical songmaster for one of the festivals. Jewish tradition and practice assigns it to the Feast of the Trumpets. Some have suggested that since both new moon and full moon are mentioned (3), the song may have been sung also at the Feast of Tabernacles which began a fortnight later. It is also suggested, with some plausibility, that the style might indicate the same author for Pss. 77; 105. There is the same abrupt ending as if a fanfare of trumpets and silence concluded the song at its height. There is the same prominence of Joseph as a name for the people. The theme of the Egyptian captivity is common to this and the earlier psalms in this decade, and may have suggested the grouping.

Commentary

1–4 There is material here, which need not concern us, for the student of religious music. The full moon feast, that of the Tents ('tabernacles'), was separated from the New Year celebration with the Great Day of Atonement in between (that is the first day of Tishri, the tenth day, and the fifteenth to the twenty-first or second of the same month). Hence the special holiness which Josephus attributes to the Feast of the Tabernacles. The rabbis said that one who had not witnessed this festival did not know the ultimate meaning of joy. Plutarch unkindly remarked that, in his day, it resembled a bacchanalian orgy, but we have no further evidence for the deterioration of the festival. Such corruption can take place at the heart of religion as the first letter to Corinth indicates. In all the more joyous celebrations of religion, dignity, reverence and order are safeguards to be recognized and cultivated.

5 Joseph is used as a patronymic for Israel because the Egyptian bondage is to become the theme. Joseph was the chief man of the land when Egypt became the home of the patriarchal family. He was 'the crowned one among his brothers' (Gen. 49.26). It is also possible that the psalmist was from the northern kingdom.

6–16 God now speaks in prophetic language of all He has done for His people and of their scant gratitude, obstinacy and judgement. The musical accompaniment probably made the intervention of the divine voice of reminiscence (6,7), asseveration (8–10), appeal (11–13) and promise (14–16) intensely dramatic.

Conclusion

The psalm is a little elusive to Gentile ears. It is almost as if a stranger had intruded on a scene of Jewish worship, the strange wailing of the trumpets, the crescendo of music and of theme, the simulated voice of Jehovah the Most High, and the whole pattern of prophetic condemnation, warning, yearning love, and apocalyptic promise. It is a psalm which must always have meant much to devout Jews.

Read Psalm 82; Amos 5; John 10.34–38

Occasion and author

Neither can be guessed. Corruption in court and the difficulty of finding uncorrupted justice and judges of invincible integrity is an old problem in the Middle East. We cannot therefore attach this psalm to any particular time or person. Amos, Micah, Isaiah, Jeremiah, Zechariah likewise attacked the courts and administration of justice. The old Hebrew passion for impartial justice pervades the prophets and this psalm might properly belong to the prophetic age, though the old direction to judge without favour goes back to Deuteronomy.

Commentary

1 The solemn responsibility of being a judge of men is set out in the opening verse. Solomon's throne is called 'the throne of the Lord' (1 Chron. 29.23), and the majesty of the judge's calling and responsibility goes back to the days of the giving of the law.

2–7 These verses purport to be the direct words of God in rebuke to a debased judiciary. Lev. 19.15; Deut. 1.17; Prov. 24.23 are only a few of the passages which stress the equality of man before the Law. 'The poor and needy', as we have had earlier occasion to remark, had scant chance of justice in the East, where a corrupted view of God set the dispossessed in a class apart, God-forsaken and therefore under the disfavour of the Most High. Why then, the bent argument went, should an earthly judge grant mercy when the Lord Himself had denied it? Jehoshaphat's charge to his judges (2 Chron. 19.7) reads curiously like this psalm. The similarity of language suggests quotation and may indicate an earlier date. No society or community can hope to maintain its superstructure, when the foundations of righteousness which buttress its strength, unseen beneath, are themselves shaken (6). And yet God has, he affirms, invested them, mere men, with His own power, life and death, and judgement over sin. This was the passage the Lord used (John 10.34–38) in ironical refutation of the Pharisees' criticism of His claim to be God's Son. 'And the Scripture cannot be broken' was a gently ironical repetition of His opponents' continual harping on an accepted fact now turned with subtlety against them.

Conclusion

Anglo-Saxon tradition stands for utter integrity in the administration of the law. It is worth noting again, in view of some shattering scandals, that all such integrity is based on a lofty view of God and a proper sense of humble responsibility on the part of those who take upon themselves the exercise and application of the sanctions of the law. Without such faith the foundations crumble and illustrations abound. 'God stands up to open heaven's court. He pronounces judgement on the judges', runs the Living Bible's felicitous rendering of the opening verse. All who hold authority over men must bear in mind that some such scene will one day be reality . . . 'In death you are mere men. You will fall, as any prince, for all must die' (LB). 'Stand up, Lord God, to dispense justice on earth.'

Read Psalm 83; reread Psalm 2

Occasion and author

It is not possible to find in the historical records such a menacing combination of frontier foes (6,7,8). Israel today must find the psalm strangely moving. From the Gaza coastlands to Lebanon (7), along all the eastern marches, with the desert reservoir of enemies, the noise of war was growing (6,8). If Gebal is indeed Byblos, and Asshur is the already emerging power which, in its final imperial strength, was to curse the Middle East for centuries, the encirclement of hate seemed frightening indeed. T. E. Lawrence, in the First World War, revealed what an elusive menace the people of the desert ('the tents of Edom') could be. In 2 Chron. 20 an eastern coalition thrust into Judah, and camped as near as Engedi, on the west side of the Dead Sea. But the attack envisaged in this psalm appears to have involved stronger and more powerfully organized states. Tyre was the centre of Phoenician power – a military and naval empire. The Philistines were still untamed and Assyria a force in politics but not yet, clearly, a first-class power. These are the only aids if an attempt to fix a date is made. Certainly the list seems to rule out a proposed Maccabean date. A map is essential if the background of this psalm is to be understood.

Commentary

1–8 The nations of the borderlands, from ancient times until today, have found it difficult to achieve unity in peace or war. Hatred of Israel brought about their brief alignment (2), inspired their crafty plans (3), the frank policy of genocide (4), and the rare concord (5) of Semitic and European peoples (6,7) – the Philistines were European. There is a similar situation in Nehemiah's story, and a striking illustration in 1 Macc. 5. 'The Gentiles round us have gathered to wipe us out,' write the beleagured garrison in Gilead to the Maccabee brothers, and 'while the letter was being read, messengers with torn clothes came in from the north. "Ptolemais, Tyre and Sidon," they said, "and all heathen Galilee, have mustered to make an end of us."'

9–12 The familiar appeal to history follows. No nation was as aware of its historic past and the significance of events, as the Hebrew people. The choice of illustration is interesting. Sisera was the head of a confederation of Canaanite kings routed by Barak and Deborah beside the flooded Kishon under the Carmel Range (Judg. 4.1–22; 5.19–31). Sisera, oddly enough, is a non-Semitic name, and he may have been the chieftain of a group of 'Sea People', who, at the time the Hebrews were pushing north into the Esdraelon Plain, were thrusting into the same fertile lowlands from the coast where Haifa now stands. When 'the stars in their courses fought against Sisera' Cannanite and allied resistance was at an end.

Jabin was similarly the leader of a confederacy of Canaanite rulers from Galilee. They were defeated by the waters of Merom, and the formidable fortress of Hazor destroyed. Joshua 11 is an account of this campaign. Jabin could have been, like Caesar and Pharaoh, a dynastic name, for we find another Jabin among Sisera's allies. Endor is not mentioned in the historical record, but the psalmist no doubt knew of a tradition which included this place in the story.

Although the Midianite raid is mentioned first, the war was later than the conflict with Sisera. The story is told in Judges 6 and 7. The tribesmen were from the eastern frontiers, penetrating deeply west by means of their camel 'cavalry'. Gideon pursued a remnant of the fleeing nomads as far as their home territory at Karkor in the Wadi Sirhan (8.10). Here he captured two of the chiefs named in the list of four.

They had all said: 'Let us take possession for ourselves of the pastures of God.' The result was that reversal of fortune which the Greeks found so awesome – the judgement on the sin of *hubris* or overweening arrogance.

13–18 The metaphor of the wheel (KJV) is variously rendered. The RSV has 'whirling dust', no doubt the small 'twisters' racing before the strong winds engendered in the Rift Valley of the Jordan. 'The tumbleweed', says the Jerusalem Bible. 'Leaves in a whirlwind', says NASB. Stubble blowing, the racing forest fire, complete the imagery of wild, unreasoning speed (13,14), with God like a tempest or hurricane behind them (15).

Then, curiously, comes a note not often struck in such commination. The psalmist would have the triumph of Israel fruitful in bringing Israel's very foes into subjection to the true God, or at least to demonstrate to all men that Jehovah is God indeed. Christian nations which have won wars might more frequently have 'won the peace' had there been in history more commonly the desire that the defeated foe might find the victor's God, or at least that the victor might be so clearly worthy of his victory, and the defeated so obviously the victim of his own sin, that the lesson should be plain to the whole world – that God's law cannot be broken.

Read Psalm 84; reread Psalm 42

Occasion and author

The writer of this vivid and moving little poem could have been one of the Levite minstrels ('the sons of Korah'), exiled from the task he loved, the care of the shrine of God. Caught in some tragedy of exile, or even cut off from Jerusalem by some such catastrophe as Sennacherib's invasion, he pours his home-sickness for the dwellings of God into the language and music of a psalm.

Commentary

1–4 The writer's passionate love for his Lord is consuming. The place where in happier days he had served God is so vivid in his memory that he sees in memory the sparrows and swallows flitting, as they may be seen today round the Dome of the Rock, under the eves and in the courtyards of the Temple. It is the small things which spring to mind when the heart is sick for home. Rupert Brooke thus writes of Grantchester in Berlin, 1912:

> *Just now the lilac is in bloom,*
> *All before my little room;*
> *And in my flower beds, I think,*
> *Smile the carnation and the pink;*
> *And down the borders, well I know,*
> *The poppy and the pansy blow . . .*

It is all very real. And the more so because the loved scene is still actual experience for some. The services continue, but he is not there . . . 'The living God' is an expression quite uncommon in the Old Testament but found in Matthew's and John's Gospels, in Paul's letters, four times in Hebrews, and once in Revelation.

5–7 Not only are they happy who dwell around and serve the shrine. Those who can still join a caravan and go there are blessed too, making the very highway blossom with their passing. The Valley of Baca (or the Vale of Weeping) was some gloomy pass on the route of pilgrimage which the writer has in mind, a road made brighter by the joy of those who passed that way. It is natural that mystic Christian thought should find something symbolic in the verse. The Vale of Tears, which is the world for many an afflicted soul, can be made fruitful for those who know how to transform the gloom around them. There are those, who, still in the words of poor Rupert Brooke, are 'washed marvellously with sorrow . . .'

8–12 And so to prayer, for God is no idol dwelling in the far city. He is under Heaven's canopy and over it. His temple is the earth. And mere trust (12) is as straight a path to blessedness as any road of pilgrimage to the Holy Place. The verses are a tumult of imagery. God is a shield, a much more meaningful figure in the ancient context than it can be today. The writer would rather serve God in the humblest fashion than to dwell accepted in the place where evil has its temporary habitation. God is like the sun, endowing all with life and banishing darkness. He gives all that makes life worthwhile – 'Sun to enlighten, shield to protect us, the Lord God has favour, has honour to bestow . . .' (Knox).

Read Psalm 85; Nehemiah 1

Occasion and author

The opening verse seems to demand that this psalm was written after the return from the Exile, but the general drift and tone of its supplication equally demand that it should be located in that period of poverty, tension, and sometimes of bitter disillusionment of which Nehemiah's book speaks so vividly. Why was the psalm placed here? In this group of psalms the clues which have often prompted some conclusion desert us. It seems clear from Book Five that the editors and arrangers of the Psalter had various earlier collections to incorporate. Perhaps the Asaph collection, like the Davidic group, required some filling out to a certain optimum size by the incorporation of unclassified or unallotted poems, judged worthy of inclusion. The Korah psalms were no doubt regarded as a coherent group, and could have appeared of convenient theme and size to fill out the corpus of Book Three.

Commentary

1–3 A foundation is laid for faith. God has shown Himself gracious. The captives resume their task of fulfilling a nation's destiny.

4–7 But amid what desolation! Faith staggers at the task of reconstruction and the tense story of Nehemiah is abundant illustration of the strain on the faith and energy of those who had returned in such high hopes. Was God, after all, still angry (5,6)? The suppliant longs for a theme for joy, for loving kindness, in a word, for rescue. 'Show us your loving concern, Lord, and favour us with speedy release' (Harrison). Life can be like that – the dawn, and forthwith a darkening sky. Such was Habakkuk's experience. He saw the glow, the hope, the deep happiness of Josiah's revival, the crash and collapse of the evil empire of Assyria, and then the rise of the 'successor-state' – the imperial might of Babylon.

8–13 Like Habakkuk, the psalmist listened and allowed God to speak. Let the first assumption be that God's will is peace (8). Let those who seek that peace be wise (8) and reverence Him (9). So shall four saving and cardinal virtues spring from the soil of any society (10,11). Truth is twice mentioned. 'I am the Way, the Truth and the Life', said the Lord, inserting Truth between the pattern and the reality of the life that is in Him. Thus shall the land prosper (12), thus the people live in peace (13).

Conclusion

A timely conclusion worth pondering. Is it not falsehood which corrupts the world? The psalmist, moving from despair to enlightenment, saw that truth was the essential base for all social happiness. The world is dying of lies, false promises, corrupted motives, pretence, posing – the thousand forms which falsehood takes in men and organizations of men. Tennyson's *Locksley Hall*, his optimistic poem of 1840, when the industrial age seemed about to open Paradise for men, is known as well as any poem of the great Victorian. Few quote *Locksley Hall Sixty Years After*. The poem of Tennyson's deep disillusionment was, in fact, written in 1885, only forty-five years later. Almost a century has gone but how relevant his words. Nations die for want of Truth:

> *Ah, if dynamite and revolver leave you*
> *courage to be wise,*
> *When was age so crammed with menace?*
> *madness? written, spoken lies?*

> *Nay, but these would feel and follow Truth if*
> *only you and you*
> *Rivals of realm-ruining party, when you*
> *speak were wholly true.*

> *Step by step we gained a freedom known*
> *to Europe, known to all;*
> *Step by step we rose to greatness, through the*
> *tonguesters we may fall.*

Read the psalm, then read the poem – but then read the psalm again. 'What is Truth?' asked Pilate. 'None but His loved ones know.'

86

Read Psalm 86

Occasion and author

This is the only psalm ascribed to David in Book Three. Why, it is immediately asked, should it thus appear towards the end of a book devoted to
Asaph and Korahite psalms? A careful survey of Pss. 25–28, and 54–57, will
disclose a possible reason. Some Levite minstrel culled this psalm from
Davidic sources, and set it very effectively together as a new piece. So it may
have appeared in an original Korah collection. 'God does not give originality
to every devout man,' says Maclaren solemnly, and anyone who uses the
Lord's Prayer or any Prayer Book, knows the refuge and comfort that
familiar and prepared phraseology can be. The compiler of this prayer knew
deeply the old Davidic prayers. It has been pointed out that the Lord's
Prayer itself is composed of petitions which can be matched or paralleled in
rabbinical writings. And why not? It is a Western heresy to see virtue in
novelty and special value in what is thought originality. The world could
benefit by a return to ancient wisdom.

Commentary

1–8   Here is the old link between affliction and poverty which is found so
often in the Old Testament, and the same claim to innocence. 'For I am
godly' (2, RSV) means no more than that the suppliant recognizes God's
name and sees a claim on God's help in the acknowledgement. The Hebrew
word *chasid* implies no more than that the psalmist stands in a 'covenant
relationship' with God, a basic Hebrew idea. He cries for mercy (3),
forgiveness (5), and neither plea suggests a self-righteous approach.

9–11   God, the psalmist is certain, is willing to save. Is He also able to
save? These verses state the assurance he holds that this also is true. Verse 8
does not suggest that God has feeble rivals among the deities of heathendom.
The verses are all culled from earlier Old Testament passages. The core of
the truth they hold is the old Abrahamic faith in one God, destined to be the
one God of all nations. Let God, therefore 'unite his heart', bend, in a word,
all the energies of his personality to one end, the exaltation of God's holy
name.

12–16   And this exaltation is praise for mercy given (12,13), protection
from the murderous assault of heathen men upon his life in God (14,15),
and clear insight. God is, in the psalmist's faith, marked by mercy, grace,
patience and truth. He rings the changes on these words.

17   'A token for good' (KJV), 'a heartening sign' (Harrison) . . . how often

32

the heart of man yearns for such assurance, and if the Lord's Prayer permits petition for our 'daily bread', the anxieties of the heart and mind may be rightly set before the Lord. There are times when some crumb of encouragement, some touch of God's hand, some proof of goodness in an evil world, are the bread of which a hungry spirit stands in direst need. As the hymn puts it:

> *When the way is dark and I cannot see*
> *Through the mist of His wise design,*
> *Though the darkness hide, He is by my side,*
> *With a touch of His hand on mine.*

> *There are times when tired of the toilsome road*
> *That for ways of the world I pine,*
> *But He draws me back to the upward track,*
> *With a touch of His hand on mine.*

Read Psalm 87; Isaiah 60.1–10

Occasion and author
A verse in the preceding psalm (7) prompts the placing of this small lyric at this point in the Psalter. It was probably written in the days of Hezekiah and Isaiah, when Judah became aware of a wider world, and a world open to the influence of Judah's God. The language often echoes Isaiah, though it cannot be claimed that the prophet was himself the psalmist. Rahab was Isaiah's name for Egypt (30.7; 51.9). Isaiah expresses the hope that the great pagan empires will worship in Jerusalem (19.21–25).

Commentary
1–3 The gates were a feature of any ancient walled city, not only an intricate part of the defences, but the place of concourse, of fellowship, and of the dispensation of justice. Set high on the central ridge of Palestine, Jerusalem, walls and gates, was quite spectacularly placed. The 'holy mountains' are, of course, this strong and dominating ridge of uplands.
4–6 Abruptly, as in some other psalms (14.4 and perhaps 32.8; 75.2; 81.6), the divine voice intrudes. Rahab is no complimentary name. In 89.10 it is applied to the Nile crocodile as a symbol of Egypt, the incarnation of pride and ferocity. 'Among those that know me I mention Rahab and Babylon, Philistia and Tyre, and also Ethiopia,' says the Voice. It is a strange intrusion, envisaging a surge of faith breaking into the surrounding

world and prophetic of the New Testament. The final phrase: 'This one was born there', is difficult unless it dramatizes some group of proselytes and a testimony to a distant birthplace, among ancient enemies, of some worshipper of God. The Ethiopian chamberlain of Queen Candace (Acts 8.27) could illustrate such a case. And does the next verse suggest a regeneration, a recognition of the Holy City as a second birthplace, by those who found a new faith, and an entry (6) into God's Book of Life? Maclaren puts it well: 'The vision of a universal Church, a brotherhood of humanity, shines radiant before the seer. Other psalmists and prophets have like insight into the future expansion of the nation, but this psalm stands alone in the emphasis it places upon the idea of birth into the rights of citizenship. This singer has had granted to him a glimpse into two truths – the universality of the Church, and the mode of entrance into it by the reception of a new life.' This seems the best interpretation of the meaning of the psalm.

7   Milton's paraphrase forms a conclusion, a poetic and mystic vision of mankind united in the worship of Israel's God.

> *Both they who sing, and they who dance*
> *With sacred songs are there,*
> *In thee fresh brooks and soft streams glance*
> *And all thy fountains clear.*

It is an obscure verse but has a total impact difficult to reduce to logic. The Living Bible paraphrase may be correct: 'And in the festivals they'll sing, "All my heart is in Jerusalem." '

Conclusion

This is a lyric poem, and in lyric poetry connecting links of logical thought are sometimes omitted. It is like the vista of a mountain range, the peaks gleaming and visible, while the intervening valleys are clothed in mist. Such is the style of this difficult psalm. It is clearly a vision of some New Jerusalem with citizenry as wide as man. Obscurity is encountered only when the speakers in the poem are sought. It is as though some directions for production are missing. The Sons of Korah no doubt understood.

Read Psalm 88; Job 3

Occasion and author

'This,' wrote Bishop Perowne, 'is the saddest, darkest Psalm in all the Psalter. It is one wail of sorrow from beginning to end. It is the only Psalm in which the expression of feeling, the pouring out of the burdened heart before God, fails to bring any consolation.' The last word is 'darkness'. The only light is in the first line; 'O God of my salvation' (KJV). That such a name could be given the Lord God at least puts purpose into the prayer and one thin gleam of hope. Older commentators avoided the difficulty of a lamentation so dire and unrelieved, by attributing to it a prophetic role in Gethsemane or in the darkness on Calvary. No such facile explanation satisfies. Here is the record of soul in agony. Perhaps Heman the Ezrahite was the author of Job, and this psalm is a chapter from his tribulation. If the psalms, in God's intention, are to reflect the gamut of human experience, it is proper that the book should contain the record of an hour so dark that no relief can come.

Commentary

It seems impossible to break up this cry of pain into sections. It had none, and Maclaren's marking of a significant division at the three points where the suppliant directly addresses God is quite artificial. The strength of the utterance lies in its very disorder.

Certain themes may be disengaged. Observe the Job-like attitude to death (3–6, 10,11,13). See Job 10.21,22. Compare also the betrayal of friends (8) who, like 'Job's comforters' saw no spectacle of pity in the afflicted man, but only the just object of wrath (Job 3.23; 13.27; 19.13–19; 20.10).

There is the desolating conviction that God was actively and inexplicably chastising him (7). It is absolutely imperative for spiritual and mental health, for the sufferer, then as now, to distinguish between what God permits and what God initiates. God can never do other than that which is good, and if He allows unexplained agony to befall, it can only be in the certain outcome of good. Patience, endurance and a determined faith may be needed before God's plan of blessing takes shape and visibility, but, if God be good and God be wise, no other explanation of unmerited suffering can satisfy or indeed be acceptable. 'Darkness is my one companion left,' runs the last clause in the Jerusalem Bible. And such is the case if no distinction between the directive and the permissive will of God is allowed.

Christians have seen the cross. They know that God Himself is involved in all human suffering for Calvary encompassed all that evil can do. 'God was in Christ bringing the world to see what He could see' – 'reconciling the world to Himself', if you will. Christians have seen the empty tomb. They know that God's plans encompass more than this little day, and that there is another page beyond the one that closes. Indeed –

> *Our own dim life should teach us this*
> *That life must live for evermore,*
> *Else earth were darkness to the core,*
> *And dust and ashes all that is . . .*

Read Psalm 89; 2 Samuel 7.8–16; Jeremiah 22.24–29

Occasion and author

The author was Ethan, a wise man of Solomon's day (1 Kings 4.31), known as a member of the family of Zerah – of which Ezrahite is the gentilic form. 1 Chron. 2.6 speaks of Ethan and Heman of the previous psalm as 'sons of Zerah'. The time was one in which the monarchy was tottering and if the author is the wise man with whom Solomon is compared, the time of composition could have been in Rehoboam's reign when the future of the Davidic monarchy was dark. Others, giving less weight to the ancient inscription, think that the psalm was written for Jehoiachin, for whom Jeremiah wrote a lament. The royal youth came to the throne in December, 598 B.C. only to inherit a disintegrating kingdom, and reigned some three months. Nebuchadnezzar took the city in March, 597 B.C., and the pathetic king went into exile. It is possible that the psalm is composite, a review of God's mercy, with the messianic promise to David ending at v. 37, and the last fourteen verses a supplement of lamentation added by another hand. The name of Ethan, on this unprovable hypothesis could be preserved as the author of the first part while the latter part could be by a poet of Jeremiah's day. The worth of the psalm would in no way be diminished by such an assumption, and its pathos would be deepened.

Commentary

1–18 The familiar themes of the formal Hebrew hymn fill this portion, God's loving care, His promises, the witness of heaven and earth to His faithfulness, the glance back to past mercies such as the stilling of the Red Sea (9,10), the very landscape bearing testimony to His majesty (12), His justice (14) . . . The theme which emerges is that such a God can do no other than keep His covenant. His nature, demonstrated in His moral majesty, demands that He fulfil His promise; His power, evident in heaven and earth, shows that He *can* fulfil His promise. History reveals that hitherto He *has* fulfilled His promise.

19–37 And this is His promise. The section paraphrases 2 Sam. 7.8–16. The psalmist examines and confirms the call of the man chosen to be the ruler of Israel, and the manner in which David proved that covenant in trial and tribulation and found it to be true. From v. 28 the stand is taken that the covenant is absolute. There may be those who fail in worthiness, but, punished though they be, the old undertaking still holds. 'It shall stand firm while the skies endure' (37, RSV).

38 Then like a flash of lightning comes the contrast, stark in its frankness. Ibn Ezra tells of a pious Spanish Jew who would never read or listen to this psalm. Ibn Ezra himself took the closing section as a quotation. Thus the foes of the people taunted them. But Psalm 44.9–22 is very similar language, and it is the common fashion of the psalms to be frank, even downright, in laying hold of God. The passage is a fine piece of poetic rhetoric for a trampled land, and military catastrophe. Verse 45 might grimly describe poor Jehoiachin, thrust from youth into broken manhood in one short winter season. So ends the psalm and the book. 'Remember, O Lord, how thy servant is scorned; how I bear in my bosom the insults of the peoples, with which thy enemies taunt, O Lord, with which they mock the footsteps of thy anointed' (50,51 RSV). Words could hardly be more moving in their dull disappointment.

Read Psalm 90; Deuteronomy 32.1–36

Occasion and author

There is no need to deny the Mosaic authorship of this sublime poem. It has, of course, been vigorously denied, chiefly by those to whom all tradition is itself a challenge to denial, or by those who approach Hebrew literature with preconceived and dogmatic theories to which phenomena must be accommodated. Moses was educated in a literary society. Akhnaton's noble hymn to the sun probably antedated anything Moses could have written. Nor are the sentiments alien to his mind. True, he lived longer than the prescribed years of v. 10, but he was a lonely man who lived apart. Alfred De Vigny's magnificent poem on Moses turns around this point. Solitary among his own the great man prays to pass as others pass – 'Laissez-moi dormir du sommeil de la terre' . . . 'Where would you that I take my steps, must I live ever mighty and alone? Let me sleep the sleep of earth . . .'

37

Tennyson caught that melancholy of age in his poem on Tithonus, the man who could not die, envying, as he roamed the shining palaces of dawn,

> *'the happy men that have the power to die,*
> *And grassy barrows of the happier dead.*
> *Release me and restore me to the ground . . .'*

The imagery, which could be paralleled from Horace to Housman, is true to one who spent half a lifetime in the unchanging wilderness watching where 'the aching berg props the speckless sky', watching the fragile grass, the changeless crags, the power of sun and storm.

The supreme greatness of Moses should be recognized. Churchill, who suffered the same sad, cleansing, empowering process of what Toynbee called 'withdrawal and return', has a forgotten essay on the theme. He recognized a kinship. But Moses possessed, far more deeply than Britain's great leader, an overwhelming consciousness of God. 'There is no reference to the desert,' says one critic, urgent for reasons to reject the Mosaic authorship. In fact, the whole psalm vibrates with the consciousness of exile and of wandering.

Commentary
1 'Lord, You have been our shelter in all ages', Harrison renders. The word occurs in Deut. 33.27, and the thought would be peculiarly attractive to a nomad people, canopied by the sky in the inhospitable desert . . .
2 . . . the inhospitable desert where nothing changes, where day by day the same shapes cut the heavens, the same play of light and shade from purple hills to crimsoned sky.
3 And man amid such cosmic symbolism of eternity seems small, transient and frail, so soon turned back to the windblown dust from which he came (so RSV, JB and others, sustaining the imagery).
4–6 So meaningless is what man calls time to the Eternal One. The coming and going of man were like the flash floods in the wadi, filled with roaring water from some far cloudburst in the distant hills only to empty again, like the soft and tender grass which sprang to life after such harsh watering, only to wither and crumble under the ruthless sun.
7–11 And why? Were they not nomads in the wilderness, exposed to the cruel climate because they had held back in fear from entry into a gentler land? The leader took upon himself the load of what he felt to be the judgement of God upon his people. And is not this supremely true of Moses willing vicariously to bear, in some prefiguration of Christ, the burden of his people's weakness and sin? Observe his poignant words, the broken sentence of Exodus 32.32. He had seen them fall by the desert track, or stumble on, frail by privation through brief years of precarious old age (10).
12 Nothing is without a purpose. God permits suffering not in idle and fruitless retribution, but in order that vital lessons may be learned. 'To suffer is to learn,' said Aeschylus, the greatest of the Greek tragedians, and Moses is anxious that wisdom should be woven into his people's consciousness by what they had passed through, that their history should have significance. 'Teach us then how to interpret our existence that we may acquire a discerning mind' (Harrison).

13 Thus purged he can pray. It was as if God had gone away and forgotten. 'Return, O Lord, you who were once with us, come back and be with us again.' The cry is one of deep distress, wrung from a noble heart by love for others, and the stress of leadership.

14,15 How long, O Lord, how long? – the common cry of the psalms. Let some dawn of history break and lift this gloom, and give us recompense for the years of pain, that 'the sight of the Rose, the Rose, may pay for the years of Hell' – as Masefield makes his weary knight say, stumbling down the last dell, still in search of the Grail.

16,17 Perhaps Alfred de Vigny imagined the scene aright. Moses stood on Nebo sharp against the sky. The beauty of evening lay across the marshalled tents. Awed, afraid before the splendour of God, the people waited and 'bientôt le haut du Mont reparut sans Moïse' – 'soon they saw the mountain's top again, and Moses was not there'.

Conclusion

A piece of poetry indeed. No great hope breaks through to lighten melancholy. As Housman wrote translating the Latin of Horace:

> *But oh, whate'er the sky-led seasons mar,*
> *Moon upon moon rebuilds it with her beams*
> *Come we where Tullus and where Ancus are,*
> *And good Aeneas, we are dust and dreams.*

Save for a noble care for generations to be born into a brighter dawn, Moses has little more of livelier hope to give. How golden is the hope which came with Christ and the empty tomb! The sheer valour of those ancient saints who carried on without a clear and certain hope of immortality is most moving to see.

But this psalm stirs the spirit, too, with its revelation of a lonely man. Most of those who have fought a good fight have been aware of this cross. That is what Mary Whitehouse called it in her diary: 'This is the Cross – to realize that there is no glamour, no appreciation to be asked or expected, nothing but ridicule, pain and loss. Friendship there is, and love, but even this does not touch the central core of loneliness in a battle of this kind. It is in this loneliness, and in this alone, that one finds Christ . . .'

So Moses found God.

91

Read Psalm 91; Job 5.1–27

Occasion and author

Neither is known. There is a beautiful metaphor from Deuteronomy
(32.11), and words resembling those of Eliphaz the Temanite, but neither
parallel suggests an author. They could only mean that a man of deep
spiritual experience, poetic gifts and understanding of the Scriptures, made
this great contribution to the Psalter.

Commentary

1 'They sit in secret looking over wasted lands,' says Tennyson of the with-
drawn and careless gods of Epicurus. Readers of English literature, from the
sixteenth to the nineteenth centuries, do well to remember that the writers'
minds were steeped in Latin. This is especially true of the Bible, of Milton, of
Pope and of Tennyson. *Secretus*, in Latin means 'set apart', 'divided', not
necessarily hidden, though that concept often naturally follows. The 'secret
place' of God is the 'abiding place' of John 14, where *mansiones* or 'places in
which to find shelter', occurring in Latin versions, led the Latin-minded
translator astray and set 'mansions' in the text of the KJV. The 'abiding
place' of the Most High is the place of His shadow. Abiding, as Godet put it,
is 'that continuous act whereby we lay aside all that which we might derive
from ourselves to draw all from Christ by faith.' God's refuge is the sense of
His all-powerful presence, grasped by faith. From the turmoil of life, the
suffocating siege of godless society, the Christian can always slip away to the
shadow of the rock, the quiet refuge of which the godless world is unaware.
The shadow of a rock means rest, refreshing, 'from the burning of the noon-
tide heat and the burden of the day'. The verse contains no repetition, as a
commentator as sensitive as Maclaren imagines. It means: 'He who retreats
to Him who is above all others, finds in His omnipotence, life in a world of
arid death, relief from the ruthless buffeting of life, and rest from the weariness of the journey of our days.'
2 The statement of the spiritual truth is followed without pause by an
expression of determination to act upon it. Truth pauses in the seat of
thought unless it is allowed to flow into the will, and the will to determine
action.
3 Likewise the expression of acceptance and committal inspires the assurance to others. No one can inspire or persuade a second person to go further
than he is prepared to go himself. 'The snare of the fowler' is some 'treacher-

ous lure' (Knox) and establishes the metaphorical nature of the guarantees of security which fill the psalm.

4 Few beasts of the field or birds of the air would have the hardihood to seek to pluck the eagle's fledglings from beneath the mighty bird's protecting wings. And truth can be a buckler. Lies certainly cannot cover up, as more than one notorious scandal of recent years has made shockingly obvious. Utter candour in conduct is always the path of safety, but the verse means more than this. A true relationship with God, a committal which flows into thought, attitude, speech, character and all one's mode of life, is the best shield against all the real harm which life can do.

5–7 The verses cannot mean that no child of God has ever been struck down in the treachery of the darkness, or swept to death in overwhelming pestilence. Arrow and bullet have found the Christian. What the verses truly mean is that, although God does not always intervene miraculously to preserve from physical peril, the man of triumphant faith, confident that his life is hidden in God, and that the brief day of earth is only part of a mightier whole, need not be lost in demoralizing fear. It is a high ideal, not the Moslem's *kismet* but the courage of Christ.

8–10 It is true that a godly way of life automatically finds shelter from some evils, but such is the wickedness of the world that it attracts others. What is, after all, meant by evil? Our estimates differ from those of the Most High, and shall we, any of us, deny that there are devils we fear more than death and the body's pain? The Lord bade us fear only that which can damage and damn the soul.

11,12 The Lord in His temptation set the pattern for the interpretation of this psalm. It was part of the Tempter's guile to trick Him into a literal experimentation with these words. Matthew 4.6 omits the words 'to keep you in all your ways.' Luke 4.10,11 omits 'in all your ways'. Satan was deliberately misquoting. The 'ways' in the psalm are obviously not the ways of earth, the paths, tracks, roads of the wilderness and city. They were the ways of obedience, duty and God's will, the ways of any who like the speaker have found the secret place of the Most High and wish to tread the tracks of His perfect will. As Calvin remarked on this verse, Satan is 'satis acutus theologus' – a 'sharp enough theologian'.

13 Confidently, then, following the Lord's own pattern of interpretation, the dangerous creatures of the pathway, sudden, strong, treacherous in their attack, need carry no fear for the Christian. Joseph found a serpent in the track when he went innocently into Potiphar's house. He trod it under foot.

14–16 God answers, and concludes the psalm. Among the translators Moffatt alone seems to give due weight to the final words. 'To show' in Hebrew is a causative form of the verb 'to see'. 'I will cause him to see how I can save'. In the context of his personal experience the man who has made God his retreat, refuge and abiding place will discover from his own un-folding circumstances that God's preserving power is real, no vain hope, no wishful imagining, but a demonstrable reality, too closely woven into events to be explained on naturalistic principles.

Conclusion

The psalmist sets a high ideal, but it is one which, in such evil times as those in which we live, we should seek to reach. John wrote Revelation in such days to show the certainty of victory. We have quoted G. K. Chesterton's *Ballad of the White Horse* in these musings. The canto which tells how Alfred, in the guise of a Wessex minstrel, sang to the jarls in the Danish camp, touches the same story. The harp went round and the pagan chiefs sang the songs of blood and death which their surviving sagas illustrate. Then Alfred seized the harp and heaved it high and the strings sparked under his touch:

> *On you is fallen the shadow,*
> *And not upon the Name;*
> *That though we scatter and though we fly,*
> *And you hang over us like the sky,*
> *You are more tired of victory,*
> *Than we are tired of shame.*
>
> *Your lord sits high in the saddle,*
> *A broken-hearted king,*
> *But our king Alfred, lost from fame,*
> *Fallen among foes or bonds of shame,*
> *In I know not what mean trade or name*
> *Has still some song to sing.*
>
> *And the king with harp on shoulder,*
> *Stood up and ceased his song*
> *And the owls moaned from the mighty trees,*
> *And the Danes laughed loud and long.*

They laugh still – but read the poem.

Read Psalm 92; reread Psalm 52

Occasion and author

The writer is unknown, but, like the writers of many of the anonymous psalms in this section of the Psalter, he must have been a man steeped in the language of Israel's hymns (for example Pss. 37,52,73). The psalm is perhaps placed here because of some similarities of language and imagery with its immediate predecessors (8). The occasion could have been the news of a victory over some old foe of the land, such as the Persian capture of Babylon. This can only be guesswork. The psalm is set down as a 'hymn for the Sabbath', and it is a fact that it is so prescribed in the Levitical order of service. A rabbinical tradition, of a more fanciful sort, says that the psalm was sung on awakening by the First Man, on the morning of the Sabbath. He had been created on the evening of the day before, our Friday, when the Sabbath, of course, in Jewish practice began.

Commentary

1–3 A prelude which calls the choir to order and sets the music in motion. It can only be imagined what the temple choirs and the stringed accompaniment must have been like. The Hebrews, of all peoples, sanctified music, and the content of their sacred songs could be profitably observed by the producers of the current spate of religious music.

4–6 There is nothing in the verses which demands a demonstration of divine power in some historic act of judgement. Indeed, v. 6 seems to suggest a more elusive manifestation of God's action in the world. The psalmist dismisses the crude and carnal man as blind to the beauties and subtleties of God's doings which are clear to the eye of insight and of faith:

> *A primrose by the river's brim*
> *A yellow primrose was to him*
> *And nothing more . . .*

Unused faculties die. Darwin once complained that he had lost the power of enjoying music. He had, he wrote, 'become a withered leaf for everything except science'. This is no necessary corollary of scientific study. Indeed, of all people, the scientist should stand amazed at the wonder of created things. It was Plato who remarked that the beginning of all understanding was wonder. The capacity to wonder sets man apart from the beast and classifies those who quench it as 'brutish' (6).

7–9 Man, puny, transient, is set in contrast, as he is so often in Hebrew thought, with the greatness of Almighty God. If, indeed, it is possible to link this composition to the fall of Babylon, these verses would gain striking force. The fall of Babylon, like the fall of Assyria's Nineveh, were events of tremendous significance in ancient history. The shock-waves of those vast historic judgements can be felt in Isaiah and Nahum.

10 Whatever inspired the verses contrasting man and God, the psalmist sensed a surge of strength and confidence. The mythological unicorn (KJV), based on the rhinoceros, came into European literature, it appears, some four centuries before Christ. It came into the Bible by way of the Septuagint, where it is called 'the one-horned', an odd mistake in translation, for the Hebrew word (*re'em*) is also used at Deut. 33.17, where the 'horns' (plural) of the 'unicorn' are mentioned. The reference is almost certainly to the wild ox (RSV), or aurochs, a huge species of oxen which died out in the fifteenth century. In the Old Testament it is usually, as in this verse, a poetic symbol of strength (cf. Num. 23.22) or fierceness (Psa. 22.21). 'You have raised me up,' says the exultant psalmist, 'until I feel the might of the wild ox in me . . .'

11 The RSV takes the glint of satisfaction out of the verse: 'My eyes have seen the downfall of my enemies, my ears have heard the doom of my evil assailants.' Moffatt accentuates the comment: 'I feast mine eyes upon my defeated foes. I hear with joy my enemies' doom.' Only those with long, agonizing personal experience of vicious cruelty and the foul barbaric torments that man can inflict on man, are free to comment on the spirit of these words. The great northern empires had hung for centuries like a dark and poisonous cloud over the lands of the Middle East. Babylon, if Babylon's fall is envisaged here, had soaked the land and the long desert tracks to the Euphrates with the blood of innocents. Let those who have themselves endured such treatment and have victoriously forgiven tyrant and tormentor, write upon such fragments of 'taunt songs' such as this.

12–15 The palm, tall, straight, fruitful in the land, was one of the most valued of trees. Its dates provided food, its leaves provided mats, its fibre thread and rigging for boats. Jericho was known as the City of Palms, and Bethany means the House of Dates. The tree is a fitting symbol for an upright, useful man, rich in worth to life's end (14). So is the cedar, the strongest and most magnificent (Ezek. 31.3–5) of the forest trees of the Eastern Mediterranean. The word 'cedar' is said to derive from an Arabic word meaning 'power'. Its magnificent timber, its fragrance, and its enduring life (it numbers millennia like the Californian redwood, and the New Zealand kauri) make the symbol of the tree singularly apt when the psalmist has in mind the worth and strength which God can give to man. The palm reaches full fruitfulness at forty years of age and then continues to bear for a century and a half. Those who have known God for forty years should go on with zest and excitement.

Verse 13 need not imply that the trees grew in the Temple precincts. Where is there a place that is not the court of God?

Conclusion

Let this be Maclaren's eloquent comment on the closing verse. It is, he says, 'a reminiscence of Deut. 32.4 . . . a final avowal of the psalmist's faith, the last result of his contemplation of the mysteries of Providence. These but drive him to cling closer to God as his sole refuge and his sure shelter, and to ring out *this* as the end which shall one day be manifest – that there is no least trace of unrighteousness in Him.'

93

Read Psalm 93; Revelation 19.11–16

Occasion and author

This is one of a group of anonymous psalms which praise God as King. Verse 8 of the preceding psalm suggests the juxtaposition and verbal links run through the series of seven psalms. Psa. 94 seems at first reading to break the sequence, but v. 8 picks up 92.6, and the psalm is a hymn celebrating royal providence and speaking doom on rebels against the throne. The theme 'Jehovah is King' runs to Psa. 99 and Psa. 100 closes the series. We seem to see the ghost of an original collection incorporated into the final corpus of the Psalter – a phenomenon which will be encountered again in the remaining psalms. The time of writing could well be the years after the return from exile when God appeared again to have ascended His throne.

Commentary

1,2 Stability, whatever the occasion, seemed to have returned to life. It was like a coronation day with the King of kings, robed in splendour, resuming rule and guidance of His own. It was one of those rare dawns in which it was good to be alive.

3,4 The scenery, the landscape of the poet's meditation, are entangled with the words, as scenes of Patmos mingled with the language of John's Apocalypse. He too was aware of the noises of the sea, and Christ's voice, as that strange vision opened, was 'as the sound of many waters', as the prisoner on Patmos remembered. One could picture the psalmist on the beach at Ashkelon looking at the long wave-beaten coast, noisy with its surf, curving north to Tel Aviv. All along that open coast the land confronts the eternal assault of the Mediterranean with unending sound that makes the voice of man sound small and thin. The poet of the psalm throws his passing thought into words ... 'Mightier than the thunder of many waters, mightier than the waves of the sea, the Lord is mighty.'

5 Here, perhaps, is an indication of the post-exilic nature of this psalm. The words might have been from the collection which forms the longest of the psalms. They reflect that new fervour for the Word which was born of the exile and one of the fine fruits of that period of cruel suffering ... And if the Temple, burned and desecrated by the cruel invaders was rising, or was soon to rise again, the mind might indeed revert to the holiness which must mark its coming. '*Your* house is left unto you desolate,' said Christ Himself to those who had made God's house *their* house, and the habitation of hucksters and of thieves.

Conclusion

For us, with whom the imagery of royalty and thrones conveys little of the notions of power and majesty which the same metaphor brought to the mind of ancient peoples, the message of the psalm is the lordship of Christ. His absolute supremacy is still a thought which a Christian must entertain and weave into the conduct of his life. 'How great Thou art . . .' should fill the truly committed mind with awe.

Read Psalm 94; Revelation 20.11–15

Occasion and author

It is tempting to regard this psalm as a psalm of David, as indeed the Septuagint maintains it is, inserted for some reason into this sequence. This could have been done with some deliberation if we were dealing here with a post-exilic group of psalms gathered round the thought of God the King. God the Judge is not remote from that thought, for in ancient contexts the king was the chief dispenser of justice in the realm. Nor was the period of reconstruction in the land one of unclouded joy, triumphant faith and united endeavour, as both historical and prophetic writings from the years after the return from captivity abundantly show. It may be assumed that whoever arranged the Psalter, or that earlier collection which was incorporated into the Psalter, had a reason in the experiences of the day, for setting a Davidic poem precisely here. Perhaps it was some Amos or Micah, some 'village Hampden' withstanding the petty tyrants of his day.

Commentary

1,2 'God of vengeance' (RSV) springs passionately into the text. It is twice repeated, and the word is plural in the Hebrew ('vengeances') as though wrongs and evil, manifest and clamant, called for the Lord to burst forth in glittering armour. It is only a diminished view of evil which shrinks squeamishly from the power of this phrase. As Maclaren puts it: 'There are times when no thought of God is so full of strength as that He is a "God of recompences", as Jeremiah calls Him (51.56), and when the longing of good men is that He would flash forth and slay evil by the brightness of His coming.' If Maclaren could say that in the days of the Pax Britannica, how much more sharply comes the thought, the longing, to our century, which has seen inhumanity and ruthless wickedness on a scale no period of history can parallel. 'The proud' are those which stir the fire of the psalmist's anger, those who assert their will in utter disregard for the life of others, men of blood, contemptuous of the weak, blasphemous, arrogant. If it is God's sovereign function to beat down such presumption there is nothing improper in a good man begging God to exercise such a right. 'Vengeance is mine and I will repay' bids man refrain from taking action unprescribed by His decree. It need not preclude the hope, the ardent hope, that judgement be not long delayed.

3–7 Justice to the weak and the afflicted was a common theme of the prophets. Such social conscience was a major contribution of the Old Testament to religion; Isa. 1.23; Amos 5.10–12; Jer. 22.3; Mic. 3.1–3 and a score of other passages illustrate the point. The psalmist uses burning words of scorn and anger against the cowardly oppressors of the weak, defenceless and small. He can only believe that God means nothing in their minds. ' "The Lord isn't looking," they say, "and besides, he doesn't care" ' (LB). This brand of practical atheism was that of the Epicureans in later centuries than the psalmist's. They believed in supernatural beings in logical accordance with a theory of physics vital to their system, but postulated that the beings whose existence they accepted had no care for men. These verses are the cry of tormented faith which sounds like impatience but is sanctified by the fact that it turns in confident expectation to God, and not in frustrated bitterness away from Him.

8–11 In splendid scorn he shows such witless creatures the folly of their assumption. Once admit the existence of a Creator and it follows that the Creator cares. If, as John 1.1 maintains, a Great Intelligence which communicates ('the Word') is behind the Universe, that Intelligence cannot be less than Love. To fall short of Love is to contain Evil and Evil destroys itself. The futility ('vanity', 11, KJV) of all atheistic thinking is demonstrable because it inevitably moves towards self-destruction. It is impossible to view the world or man, or anything else in true perspective unless the point of view is God's. It is impossible to omit a vital factor and reach a correct conclusion. That is why G. K. Chesterton, already quoted, was right when he maintained that 'it is only Christian men keep even heathen things'.

12–15 With a sudden change and a burst of compassion, the psalmist turns to the persecuted. Their suffering, permitted of God, could not, in the hands of Love and Wisdom, be fruitless. Evil finds its self-dug pit, but pain can bring a deeper and richer knowledge of God. Ultimately those two laws stand firm. Only as they operate does justice stand firm and life make sense. These four verses are the very basis of faith in a world obviously awry, where evil too often seems to triumph and justice to be denied. 'Truth, for ever on the scaffold, wrong for ever on the throne', this is the grim spectacle thrust hard against our faces. It is only as God, as Lowell's verse continues, 'standeth in the shadows keeping watch upon His own', that it becomes possible to face life victoriously. 'The future is with men of upright mind,' Moffatt renders the last phrase. The meek, the gentle, in a word, 'shall inherit the earth'.

16–19 To reach such a conclusion had called for all the courage a brave soul could muster. In the process of learning he had often felt alone (16), he had faced despair (17), but he had tried God in his last extremity, and found the Hand outstretched to save (18). And so 'amid all the thronging cares that fill my heart, my soul finds comfort in thy consolation' (19, Knox).

20–23 The closing movement of the psalm sums up the whole. Darkness and light, good and evil cannot mix. The psalmist lays that down as a basic principle, one which Paul, steeped in Old Testament thought, put into an eloquent paragraph (2 Cor. 6.14–18). Evil is a fact, visible and almost overwhelming. God is a fact only to be discovered by those who, thirsting for righteousness, endure the pain and seek for His meaning. It follows that only those who dwell in God can find meaning, purpose and ultimate peace. Evil will most surely die. The world, as John put it, with its sickening carnality and its false notions of splendour, will pass, but the man in Christ is part of an eternal reality and can never die (1 John 2.16,17).

Conclusion
Here is the full argument which faith must ever repeat. As experience multiplies behind, so it becomes more easy to believe that a Loving Presence overshadows and works all things into a pattern of good. But amid the clamour and the din of strident evil, the dark moments come when the fear that God is dead, or gone away, scrapes the surface of the mind. At which faith turns and traverses again the record, finds it true, and with lightened footstep pursues its way. 'Unless I had believed . . . oh, unless I had believed to see, here in this world, that God is good . . .' (Psalm 27.13).

Read Psalm 95; Exodus 17.1–7; Numbers 14.12–23; 20.1–13; Hebrews 4.1–10

Occasion and author
The psalm is anonymous in spite of the words 'through David' of Heb. 4.7. 'David' was a generic name for the psalms in later Hebrew thought, because of the poet-king's dominance in the earlier literature of the Psalter. There is no significance in the alleged division of the psalm into two parts. Verse 7 follows naturally enough the six verses which call to worship and the dramatic ending in which words are put into the mouth of God is acceptable literary form. If the psalm is post-exilic, it is a plea, based on history, history remote enough to be regarded in perspective, not to fail yet again. The writer was a poet and a preacher, a warm-hearted man with a deep concern lest a beloved nation fail again.

Commentary
1,2 The hymn begins with the customary call to the Levite choir to raise high the sound of song and music.
3–6 Logically there follows the call to worship and the appeal to the wonders of nature which mark this group of psalms, and evoke some splendid poetry. It is a pity that the words rendered in the KJV 'the strength of the

hills is his also', should properly be translated 'the heights'. The older version is one of those translations which seem to stand in their own right and add a phrase to the literature of another language. Many scenes of mountain grandeur invade the mind – Ben Nevis, stark above its glen, the stern northern face of the Eiger, the Wetterhorn, strong in its muscled rock above Grindelwald, Mount Cook, like a southern Matterhorn above the glaciers . . . strength is the thought the mighty snow-streaked precipices suggest. And the poet who set his love of nature so prominently into several of this group of psalms was a man who felt movingly the presence 'of something far more deeply interfused' in the sight of Hermon, Carmel, the surf-beaten coast, the herbage green after the rain. There are those who come near to God by some simple sight of beauty, and feel unbidden come the instinct to worship (6). 'Dear God, to see the branches stir, across the moon at Grantchester,' said Rupert Brooke, so soon to die in youth.

7   Anguished at the thought that others could not see as he could see, that the Lord is our shepherd, and we, helpless, witless, wandering, are His sheep, the psalmist breaks into his appeal – 'Today, oh today, listen to the voice so clear to hear.' Or is it the voice of God breaking in? 'Today if you will hear MY voice' as some read.

8–11   Do not do as your ancestors did. The miracle of God's presence was around them. Sinai set its law in their midst. God had fostered them and led them to the very place where they could grasp the promise. And then, in feebleness of faith and rebellion they set Meribah and Massah (RSV) into history. These two localities are mentioned several times together. They probably were adjacent and both were covered by the marshalled camping places of the tribes. The rebellious people challenged God and tested Him. They found that they were tested themselves, were refused the rest of Canaan, and left to wander in the wilderness they had chosen. God sometimes says to the obstinately rebellious: 'Thy will be done.'

'Cannot you see,' says the psalmist, 'you hard of heart, what history means? There is still a peace of God to find, a rest which you can choose, if you will but abandon the wandering of the wilderness.'

Conclusion

The study of this psalm can hardly be concluded without a careful reading of what the New Testament has to say on the subject. The Epistle to the Hebrews is a remarkable revelation of the working of a mind steeped in the Old Testament. It is not a pattern for common preaching today. Its thought forms and imagery are those of a Hebrew trained since childhood to think within the circle of the ancient Scriptures, and speaking to those of like mind and training.

The writer of the letter, like the psalmist, was fearful lest his compatriots should miss what God had for them in Christ, the peace of God which Christians had found, and held back, as their nomad ancestors had done, still wandering in the wilderness of Judaism. They would not listen in Moses' day. Appeals were vain. Caleb and Joshua could praise the beauty and fruitfulness of the land. None would listen or translate words into action.

The New Testament letter, as its title implies, was addressed primarily to Jewish Christians who were lapsing into an arid Judaism, but its general principles apply to all Christians. Life can be unfruitful, poverty-stricken and incomplete if the fullness of God's salvation is not grasped. Fear, feebleness of faith, an unsurrendered will, can hold back a life which might be powerful for God, and confident in its witness, from the wealth which one step across a frontier of the mind can take at any moment. Such is the lesson for us. The fine words of a Keswick hymn touch the thought well:

> *My Saviour, Thou hast offered rest:*
> *O give it then to me;*
> *The rest of ceasing from myself,*
> *To find my all in Thee.*
>
> *This cruel self, O how it strives*
> *And works within my breast,*
> *To come between Thee and my soul,*
> *And keep me back from rest.*
>
> *How many subtle forms it takes*
> *Of seeming verity,*
> *As if it were not safe to rest*
> *And venture all on Thee.*
>
> *In Thy strong hand I lay me down,*
> *So shall the work be done:*
> *For who can work so wondrously*
> *As the Almighty One?*

Read Psalm 96; 1 Chronicles 16

Occasion and author

The Septuagint has a somewhat contradictory heading for this anthem of praise. It speaks of it as a psalm for the second Temple, 'after the Captivity', and also ascribes it to David. The Chronicler, in fact, ascribes it to David on the occasion of the restoration of the Ark to the sanctuary. There need be no contradiction. The writer of this group of psalms had three characteristics, if we guess aright. He was a poet of nature, he had a global vision of his faith, and he had learned, in exile, to value the Word. The third characteristic will appear in strength in Book Five of the Psalms. This is why this group contains masses of allusion and quotation from earlier psalms, from the prophets and, especially here, from Isaiah. Observe Isa. 35. It would appear quite natural to such a poet, his mind stored with his own rich poetic heritage of sacred verse, to lift from its earlier historic context a psalm of David, and to adapt it, with minor alterations to a later and similar occasion of religious joy. Nor would it be impossible for the later version to overlay the earlier version in successive copyings of the chapter in Chronicles. The truth or authority of the passage in both contexts would in no way be lessened.

Commentary

1–3 The first of the three strophes opens with a call to worship the King of kings, a thought stressed in the New Year festival. 'Bless his name' means 'praise Him for being what He is', just as 'believe on His name', means 'believe He is what He claims to be'. 'Never cease to bear record of his power to save' (2, Knox). Verse 3 turns to the pagan world. The evangelical touch is not as sharply clear as it sometimes is, but a note is sounded which will gather strength in this portion of the Psalter.

4–6 The second half of the first strophe stresses the old Abrahamic vision of One God. Verse 4 does not concede being to the deities of paganism but the writer, like the early Christians, might conceivably have accepted the existence of certain malign powers, fallen angels or the like, who claimed the worship of idolators, and held a certain evil power over them. 'All the gods of the nations are nothings,' runs v. 5. The word literally means vain or empty things. 'Idols' have no content, no power to save, and seen closely they disappear. 'Idol', after all, means no more. It is the Greek for an 'appearance', and in Epicurean phraseology is a mere film of atoms, impalpable, insubstantial, though capable of impinging on the eye and creating an image. The notion of a graven image was a derived one. But the true God – 'His presence is one of splendour and majesty, praise and glory are found in His shrine' (Harrison).

7–9 'O nations of the world, confess that God alone is glorious and strong,' runs the Living Bible paraphrase of v. 7, and the next verse moves boldly to an invitation to come and worship in His Temple. Verse 9 may mean 'worship the Lord in holy array' (RSV), 'in sacred vestments' (Moffatt) even 'in a sanctified spirit' (Harrison), but the KJV's 'in the beauty of holiness' has happily put a beautiful phrase into the English language. J. S. B. Monsell (1811–1875), vicar of Guildford when he died, wove those words into a magnificent hymn, worthy of the psalm from which its theme was taken . . .

> *O worship the Lord in the beauty of holiness,*
> *Bow down before Him, His glory proclaim;*
> *With gold of obedience, and incense of lowliness,*
> *Kneel and adore Him, the Lord is His Name.*
>
> . . . . .
>
> *Fear not to enter His courts in the slenderness*
> *Of the poor wealth thou wouldst reckon as thine;*
> *Truth in its beauty, and love in its tenderness,*
> *These are the offerings to lay on His shrine.*

10–13 A four verse strophe closes the hymn and the writer's love of nature breaks into the theme, the roar and amplitude of the sea throwing itself upon the ramparts of the land, the smiling countryside, and the woodlands, where the leaves, turning and flashing in the bright breeze seem to spell rejoicing. 'One impulse from a vernal wood', as Wordsworth put it, can awaken thoughts beyond philosophy.

And the psalm closes with the old Isaian vision of the Coming King.

Conclusion

Need anything more be said? There is an exquisite completeness about these psalms. The words might still be sung, in worship, in appeal to a still enveloping paganism, with an invitation still as relevant to a soiled and contaminated world to come to the Lord 'in the beauty of holiness'.

But observe too how the mind's preoccupation with noble thoughts and exalted language can form and shape a prayer. This psalm is a mosaic of quotation and allusion. Someone has collected the list: compare v. 1 with Pss. 33.3; 40.3; 98.1; v. 3 with Pss. 9.11; 105.1; v. 4 with Pss. 48.1; 95.3; v. 10 with Pss. 9.7,8; 98.9. And then again compare v. 2 with Isa. 52.7; v. 3 with Isa. 60.6; 66.18; v. 5 with Isa. 40.18–20; 41.24; 46.5,6,7; vs. 11–13 with Isa. 41.19; 44.23; 49.13 and a whole tract of Isa. 35. How relevant this realization is to the Lord's conversation with Nicodemus where the words of both participants can be understood if it is kept in mind that Nicodemus knew the Old Testament by heart and would appreciate the subtle play on imagery derived from Numbers, Ezekiel and Jeremiah.

> *With harps and with viols there*
> *stands a great throng*
> *In the presence of Jesus, and sing*
> *this new song:*
>
> . . . . .
>
> *He maketh the rebel a priest and a king,*
> *He hath bought us, and taught us*
> *this new song to sing:*
>
> *Unto Him Who hath loved us*
> *and washed us from sin,*
> *Unto Him be the glory for ever!*
> *Amen.*

97

Read Psalm 97; Exodus 19.9; 20.21

Occasion and author

The psalm seems to be by the same hand or hands as its predecessor. The theme is resumed and woven with new emphases. Again we have the 'mosaic' of references to other scriptures (e.g. Deut. 5.22–27; Pss. 50.3,6; 77.18; 83.18; 32.5,11; 112.4; Isa. 42.17; Mic. 1.4, not to mention the imagery of cloud and thunder).

Commentary

1-3 It is suggested that some signal judgement on paganism may have fallen, for example the fall of Babylon to the army of the Medes and Persians. The word rendered 'isles' (the word of 72.10) is common in Isaiah for 'coasts' or 'borderlands', The reference seems to be no more than a poetic allusion to other realms than Israel. The next two verses call up the imagery of Sinai, mountain symbol of God's justice, and dark with the volcanic fires which accompanied the giving of the Law.

4,5 The volcanic imagery continues with perfect tenses which indicate that an action is complete and accomplished. Sinai was an event, irrevocably set in history. And how true. No event in pre-Christian history can outweigh the significance of the giving of the Hebrew Code.

6-9 The conclusion follows. No other ancient people rose to the national consciousness of a righteous God. That sublime truth was embedded in the heart of the Hebrew contribution to the thought and civilization of man. The gods of other nations, even the brilliant Greeks, were thought of as capricious, incalculable, cruel. One could never anticipate their action. True, great souls like Socrates and Aeschylus, broke through, in the strength of pure thought, to concepts of divine holiness and to the conviction that a vast moral law operated in the sum of things, but the holiness and justice of God was so fundamental in Hebrew thinking that no 'world-view' or concept of history escaped its presence.

10 It follows that those who love God hate evil, and out of that thought a philosophy of life emerges. If a man loves God he must expect to be delivered from evil. Hence the deep conflict in the Hebrew soul. It so often happened, as it happens still, that the good appear not to be so saved. We have seen the psalms wrestle with the problem, and a partial key to the solution lies in what in God's eyes, *is* ultimate evil. Christ and Calvary are the ultimate demonstration that God Himself is involved in the enormous reality of a fallen world, and the Christian, like the greatest of the Old Testament saints, for example Habakkuk and to a lesser extent Job, found themselves forced to a stance of faith, faith that God knows, God has not abandoned His own, God has a purpose which will ultimately prove satisfying and complete.

11 The verb 'sown' probably means 'scattered'. The same effect is given by following the RSV and NEB rendering 'dawns' which probably reflects a slightly different Hebrew text. The writer's poetic approach to nature probably has in mind the high cirrus cloud catching first the flash of the yet unrisen sun, a promise in the skies of the day to be – when Aurora's team, in Tennyson's phrase, 'beats the twilight into flakes of fire'. Milton, with this psalm in mind, extended the figure to the dew:

> *Now Morn, her rosy steps in th' Eastern clime*
> *Advancing, sowed the earth with Orient pearl . . .*

12 And so the final exhortation, echoing two verses in Pss. 30 and 32.

Conclusion
Let us separate the closing words as a concluding summary. There is cause for thankfulness in the thought that God is good. The truth is too readily taken for granted. There are atheists who live out their lives in the conviction that a non-moral universe, without knowledge, without care is all that is apart from man. There are pagans who crouch lifelong in the fear that all about and over them is a malign creation. The faithful know that the Universe is kindly, and that they live under the shadow of a Great Right Hand. The conviction is that of Rom. 8.28 and if it can be apprehended in its freshness, the thought can make life rich, confident, altogether satisfying. We travel too much, most of us, with Mr. Fearing.

Read Psalm 98; Isaiah 55

Occasion and author
The Psalm is based on Psalm 96 and passages from Isaiah. Its spirit of jubilation is its own. There is no special virtue in novelty or originality. The Lord's Prayer can be paralleled by many rabbinical utterances and is no less the Lord's Prayer for that. The rich treasury of uttered truth was at hand for the psalmist to draw upon, and there was no need to alter the words which others or himself had already said in order to make them his own. The occasion was probably the restoration of Israel viewed as a judgement on the captors and the oppressors. It was no less. The historic judgement on the mighty city of the Euphrates plain, and its farflung empire came when the Persians captured the capital. That event was directly linked to the emancipation of the Jews.

Commentary

1–3 What was defeat, utter and complete for the Babylonian Empire, was 'mercy and truth' or 'steadfast love and faithfulness' (RSV) to Israel. There is no need to regard 'judgement' as something inappropriate for gratitude and rejoicing. Why not? The fall of some evil or monstrous wickedness is vindication of the moral law, and without confidence in that moral law earth is darkness indeed. As God has pledged, so God has performed.

4–6 Therefore let the people rejoice and every instrument of the Temple choir ring forth in loud praise. 'Let the earth hear.'

7–9 And if that hyperbole is to approach literal reality it requires more than a symphony of strings and trumpets to produce the music. Seas, rivers and mountains are called in to swell the storm of praise. So, in rare times of gladness, the things of nature seem to act. Jubilation pours out from the soul, too small to contain it, in such overflow that 'Heaven above is softer blue, Earth around is sweeter green'. Such exuberance is too rare in most of us, and the fact perhaps marks some defect in our faith or apprehension of the vaster truths of life. True enough, in moments of quieter musing, most Christians find that indeed 'something lives in every hue that Christless eyes have never seen', but the abandon of this psalm eludes most people. It is perhaps only those who have personally witnessed a tremendous deliverance, some V-Day of the spirit beyond compare, who can ride the torrent of such joy.

Perhaps we await in global reality the repetition of what the returning exiles saw, or the final and cosmic fulfilment of the closing verse. What joy, were the horror and menace of today to find conclusion in the Coming of the Lord! And let us remember that such a consummation, for all our inability to envisage its reality, is part of our faith and deeply embedded in the Word.

Conclusion

Read the last chapter of the Bible.

99

Read Psalm 99; reread Psalm 51

Occasion and author

This is the seventh of a series most probably from one author or compiler, which might bear Perowne's title – Royal Psalms. It is difficult, as has been obvious, completely to dissociate their themes and particular emphases, but it was natural enough that the image of royalty should dominate Jewish thought after the exile. They had suffered much at the hands of Kings – strutting megalomaniacs like the great conqueror Nebuchadnezzar, and carnal tyrants like Belshazzar, the regent of Babylon. And now the old dream of a greater monarch of David's line seemed about to be born again.

Commentary

1–3 The passing of Babylon, like the passing of Nineveh, was indeed a call to all the peoples of the world to tremble. And the call is relevant today as the stars of apocalyptic imagery fall from the sky, and as the thoughtful can look back on the debris and ruin of twenty-six recorded civilizations along the path of history. What is there save the Lord and His righeousness to preserve any people from disaster?

4,5 The first verse is awkwardly rendered in the KJV. The RSV sets it right. 'Mighty King, lover of justice, thou hast established equity, thou hast executed justice and righteousness in Jacob.' Or the Jerusalem Bible: 'You are a king who loves justice, insisting on honesty, justice, virtue, as you have done for Jacob.' Few kings of the ancient world were thus distinguished. The monsters of cruelty and blood who ruled Assyria, the mad tyrant Nebuchadnezzar, and the noisome rest, were typical of the rulers of the east. Cyrus was a good, wise king, but Persia, like its predecessors, soon produced such sanguinary tyrants as the brute who moves through the pages of Esther's story. The Jews never lost the vision of one who rules with justice. The Lord God remained the pattern.

6–9 So history, in its broad movement, as this writer saw it, showed. And the theme closes with a third affirmation of His holiness. 'Holy, holy, holy, Lord God Almighty . . .' Moses is linked with Aaron as a priest because he exercised priestly functions. He sprinkled 'the blood of the covenant' (Exod. 24). He conducted services of consecration (Lev. 8). Examples of sacerdotal functions, as mediator and intercessor, could be multiplied.

Conclusion

A thought from v. 8 might be lifted to prominence as a conclusion. It could easily be passed by in the brighter theme of the psalm. The note of retribution which closes the verse is not to be so easily passed by. Sin forgiven can still leave behind its consequences in life, in the body, in memory or in irreparable loss. The character, however, of such can be transformed. They can become the agents of humility, spurs to new endeavour, the stimuli of strength.

Read Psalm 100

Occasion and author
This psalm, next to Psalm Twenty-three the most famous of the psalms, is a sort of doxology to the 'royal psalms'. It is a true utterance with a clear vision of a faith and indeed a gospel, wider than the people of the sanctuary.

Commentary
1   This verse has been likened to a trumpet blast heard round the world and summoning all the earth to worship (98.4).
2   The summons, having called mankind to attention, is widened and directed to the Temple, where no 'Court of the Gentiles' is envisaged, but all are free to come.
3   It is just possible, so similar are two vital words (*lo* and *lo'*), that the text could read 'and we are his' rather than 'and not we ourselves'. Pronunciation would be identical. Major modern versions accept this amendment. There is however, some significance in the KJV reading. It sets in stark simplicity the alternative to believing in a Creator – the faith in a self-creating universe – not an easy faith to hold.

Nor is such a faith secure. In a lecture given in Adelaide in 1951, Professor Smart sought to shake the logical foundations of the old 'proofs' of God's existence – they never were proofs, be it noted, only demonstrations of vast probability on which faith could make intelligent choice and take its stand. Smart concludes: 'Let us ask, "Why should anything exist at all?" Logic seems to tell us that the only answer which is not absurd, is to say, "Why shouldn't it?". Though I know how any answer on the lines of the cosmological argument can be pulled to pieces by correct logic, I still feel I want to go on asking the question . . . my mind seems to reel under the vast significance it seems to have for me. That anything should exist at all does seem to me to be a matter for the deepest awe . . .' Unlike some philosophers, Professor Smart knows that there are matters which cannot be reduced to words and dismissed. He retains what Plato thought the prerequisite of all philosophy – a sense of wonder.

Nor is the cosmological argument so easily shaken by what the Australian philosopher calls 'correct logic'. There are good minds enough which find it satisfying and compelling.

4 As though the psalm were a processional, the verse envisages the gates coming into view – as in Psa. 24. It is fitting at such a moment to lift a voice of praise and worship.

5 The song pauses, as though some vast finality has prevailed, some eternity dawned. This is a universal and a timeless psalm.

Footnote

The middle years of the sixteenth century saw the first major attempt to put the psalms into English metrical form. Some of the attempts were deplorable, noted much more for piety than for poetry. This psalm has been fortunate. The year 1561 saw two editions of the English Psalter published, one in Geneva, and one in London. The former was edited by William Kethe and became the parent of the Scottish Psalter. Kethe himself was responsible for the magnificent paraphrase of Psalm One Hundred, written especially for its perfectly appropriate tune – the *Old Hundredth*. It remains the only fragment of this ancient psalter still in common use. Isaac Watts tried another version in 1719, a version revised by Wesley in 1736. Neither improved on Kethe's inspired simplicity. Scan them side by side.

All people that on earth do dwell,
Sing to the Lord with cheerful voice;
Him serve with mirth, His praise forth tell,
Come ye before Him and rejoice.

The Lord, ye know, is God indeed;
Without our aid He did us make:
We are His flock, He doth us feed,
And for His sheep He doth us take.

Oh, enter then His gates with praise,
Approach with joy His courts unto;
Praise, laud, and bless His name always,
For it is seemly so to do.

For why? The Lord our God is good;
His mercy is for ever sure;
His truth at all times firmly stood,
And shall from age to age endure.

William Kethe, 1560

Before Jehovah's aweful throne,
Ye nations, bow with sacred joy:
Know that the Lord is God alone;
He can create, and He destroy.

His sovereign power, without our aid,
Made us of clay, and formed us men;
And when like wandering sheep we strayed,
He brought us to His fold again.

We are His people, we His care,
Our souls, and all our mortal frame:
What lasting honours shall we rear,
Almighty Maker, to Thy Name?

We'll crowd Thy gates with thankful songs;
High as the heavens our voices raise;
And earth, with her ten thousand tongues,
Shall fill Thy courts with sounding praise.

Wide as the world is Thy command;
Vast as eternity Thy love;
Firm as a rock Thy truth shall stand,
When rolling years shall cease to move.

Isaac Watts, 1719
John Wesley, 1736

Read Psalm 101; 2 Samuel 7

Occasion and author

This psalm is attributed to David, and, as has been often remarked in these studies, where there is no compelling reason to reject it, an ancient tradition of authorship must be taken seriously. Why a psalm of David should stand in isolation at this point in the book is a matter for surmise. It is possible that its subject is not remote from that of the series of royal hymns which has just concluded. The poem reflects the ideals of a monarch newly crowned. David had won through to a day of deep fulfilment. The exile was over, the exile of the wilderness and the virtual exile of Hebron. His royal court was where it ought to be – on Zion, Judea's peak. There is no doubt that, on such a summit of time and place, the new king would ponder the responsibilities of kingship, and beg God to aid him in his deep desire to create a godly court. The pity is that the decay of the years mocked so much of this early prayer, and frustrated the genuine yearnings of a great man's heart. The words, none the less, still stand for all who find themselves, as men of God, in a place of influence and authority. An ideal always moves, like a guiding light, ahead of achievement.

Commentary

1 Mercy (which, as Shakespeare said, 'becomes the throned monarch better than his crown') and judgement are the two prime prerogatives of a king. Others render the first word 'lovingkindness'. The RSV is obtuse in translating 'loyalty'.

2 However the second part of the verse is rendered, it expresses a longing for the presence of God. Some maintain that this refers to the symbolic presence represented by the ark and its transfer to Zion from the farmstead of Obed-edom. It need not necessarily be thus interpreted. The psalmist was sufficiently aware of God to think of His divine presence without visible signs of divinity. There were, after all, such promises as that of Exod. 20.24.

3 In view of the fact of an awesome Presence, the writer proposes to walk with care. He will maintain 'integrity of heart' (2, RSV) or 'live an exemplary life in my own house' (Harrison). If not there, where else? 'I will set myself no sordid aim' (NEB).

He will treat with loathing all deviations from the truth ('them that turn aside', KJV). 'Crooked practice' turns the phrase well, and a betrayed and wounded public longs for such manifestation of integrity in the high places of government.

4 In a word, 'I will know nothing of evil' (RSV), 'I shall have no dealings with wrongdoing.' Thus leadership begins. The court, staff, followers, subordinates of any leader, commonly enough follow the lead given. That is a matter of observation in almost any sphere of human activity. David therefore does well in setting his own character in order first. Having thus prominently manifested the virtue he desires, he can demand it in others. The pity is that he fell short in later years.

5 The whisperer of evil, exploiting the pathological suspicions of the great, was a common denizen of the Eastern court. It was a bold, brave stroke to make such public proclamation that such whisperings must cease. Likewise banished from the royal presence are those, 'of haughty looks and arrogant heart'. Such men are unclean, too preoccupied with self to be loyal to others.

6 The vacant places are to be filled with the faithful and the blameless. Only through good men can a good ruler transmit influence and authority to the rank and file. It is the duty of any man of God in a post of leadership to recognize this fact. The goodness he contains must not be corrupted in transmission.

7 That is why he will banish from the circle of his court he who 'practises deceit and utters lies'. Utterance and action cannot be dissociated. They are aspects of expression of that which lies behind all expression – the condition of the life.

8 'Early' of the KJV is a weak rendering of what stands in the text, as most other translators acknowledge. It is this expression of 73.14 and Isaiah 33.2, and alludes to the oriental practice of holding court in the morning (Jer. 21.12; Zeph. 3.5). Ironically, the trial of Christ took place in the morning . . .

Conclusion

C. S. Lewis, who came fresh to the Psalter after his adult conversion, speaks of his surprise at finding there the prominence of sins of the tongue. 'It is all over the Psalter,' he writes. 'One almost hears the incessant whispering, tattling, lying, flattery and the circulation of rumours. No historical adjustments are here required, we are in a world we know. We even detect in that muttering and wheedling chorus voices which are familiar. One of them may be too familiar for recognition.'

102

Read Psalm 102; Hebrews 1

Occasion and author

This psalm was written, it appears, by someone who had suffered deeply in
the exile of Israel, but who now, in the very night of sorrow, saw the dawning of the day. With a tenacity which can never be other than daunting, the
Jews had held their faith, and, conceiving God as they did, were convinced
that their land must rise again and resume its destiny (12,13). Prayer so
long, so intense, a desire so rooted, so passionate must, they thought,
prevail (14–20). As often, in both the psalms of royalty and the psalms of
suffering, a vision intrudes of a coming King and a mightier restoration.

Commentary

1,2 This is a natural beginning for a penitential psalm, and among the
penitential psalms this psalm has always been numbered. Verse 2 is drawn
from half a dozen earlier psalms – a sign that old scriptures were by now the
common framework of pious thought. This is a prayer, as the ancient
heading says, of a man at the end of his tether. The mind, almost too weary
to put thought into coherent words, falls back on what has been said by
other suppliants, other sufferers.

3–11 In a mass of metaphor the psalmist describes the extremity of his
grief. The East is vocal in complaining, the West reticent. And such reti-
cence sometimes kills compassion. The words are vivid. Life passes like
insubstantial smoke, the body wastes in its heat (3). Like the dry dead grass,
all emotion is blighted within him (4). He is emaciated (5), utterly lonely
like a bird of the waste land (6) or the high bare roof (7). And worse, the
voice of scorn, the ancient world's contempt for the apparently God-forsaken (8), lies heavily upon him. His food is dry in his mouth (9), for the
unnerving and awful thought obtrudes that the scorners may be right, and
God Almighty may indeed have flung him down in wrath (10). The sun of
life is dropping to the western desert's rim. The shadows lengthen 'across
the little daytime of his life' (11).

12–22 This passage surely indicates that the prospect of return and
restoration is near. But will it come before the writer's sun is set, and the
lengthening shadows merge with the purple twilight on the desert's face,
and the night falls? God, to be sure, will sit enthroned for ever (12). His time
has come for mercy on the fallen city, symbol of Israel's nationhood (13).
The imagination of the exiles kindles at the mere thought of the jumbled
ruin heap on the Judean ridge (14). It is curious that Luther and others

61

should have complicated the meaning of this simple poignant verse. It is literally the ruin that was the holy city, the dust that was the powdered memorial of sacred buildings that the psalmist has in mind. Until comparatively recent times pious Jews had the dust of Jerusalem sprinkled on their bodies. The world will wonder (15) at such a manifest restoration (16), a prayer so notably answered (17). History was in the making and the record will make posterity glad. This is true through all the story of the centuries, both Jewish and Christian. The long suffering of the people in exile and dire captivity, assumes a wondrous significance in the context of a national rebirth (18–22).

23–28 As so often appears in the psalms, the speaker, caught for a moment in a surge of triumph, seems to fall back into the trough from which his spirit sought to rise. He fears a premature death (23), before he can be part of the new chapter he confidently believes is opening. God is eternal but man can be cut off even before the full total of his years (24). God lived long before human history began (25) and will live when the human story ends, casting off the worn and tattered centuries as a man might cast aside a worn-out garment (26). 'Thou art He,' says the Hebrew simply (27). As Luther translates: 'You remain as you are.'

Footnote

Verses 25–27 are quoted by the writer of the Epistle to the Hebrews in the context of a group of messianic passages from the Psalms. These verses are not in themselves messianic in the sense that they refer prophetically to Christ. They merely assume such significance in the pattern of the verses into which they are woven. The writer's point is that Christ was with God before the worlds began, John's point that 'without Him nothing that is was created'. His mind moved in the imagery and the language of the Old Testament scriptures, and it was natural enough, as a straight reading of the New Testament chapter demonstrates, to incorporate these verses with the description of the Eternal God and the coexistent Christ. Such quotation was felicitous, for the psalmist has spoken pre-eminently of God as Redeemer, the great restorer of the people. In Christ God was the Redeemer incarnate.

Conclusion

> *We would see Jesus – for the*
> *shadows lengthen*
> *Across this little landscape of our life;*
> *We would see Jesus, our weak faith to*
> *strengthen,*
> *For the last weariness – the final strife.*
>
> *We would see Jesus – the great Rock Foundation,*
> *Whereupon our feet were set with*
> *sovereign grace;*
> *Not life, not death, with all their agitation,*
> *Can thence remove us, if we see*
> *His face.*

*We would see Jesus – this is all we're
needing,
Strength, joy, and willingness come
with the sight;
We would see Jesus, dying, risen,
pleading,
Then welcome day, and farewell
mortal night!*

Read Psalm 103

Occasion and author
This is said to be a psalm of David. The Syriac title goes further and assigns
it to David's old age. Those who give small weight to tradition set the psalm
down as post-exilic, and assign it to the accomplished author of the fine
psalm which follows. Aramaisms in the text, if such there be, are no indication of date. They could be legitimate modernizations of the text. If allusions
to Job and Isaiah are certain, the conclusion by no means follows that the
psalm was subsequent to those two books. The argument could apply in
reverse. While continuing to admit that certainty is elusive, it may still be
said that the psalm could be from the hands of the psalmist king.

Commentary
1 Here is worship clear and strong with the whole being committed and
summoned up to praise, mind, heart, will caught up in one surge of love.
2 Memory is involved in all such worship. Memory, as Mme. de Stael
remarked, can be a joy and a scourge. To remember what God has done is a
stimulus to worship.
3 And sins forgiven are a humbling, yet sanctifying, memory. 'God's
benefits will not be before our eyes,' said Augustine, 'unless our sins be also
before our eyes.'
4 The verse almost breaks through to the concept of immortality. When
life is adorned with God's love and pity a sort of royal glory is set upon it.
5 The satisfaction of a soul at rest, the sense of rebirth like the legendary
eagle's, are the blessings of a living faith.
6 A confidence in the ultimate vindication of righteousness is the deepest
aspiration of man. Many a psalm cries aloud for it. So do we, faced with the
horrors of the century. It is within the grasp of the psalmist's faith.
7 For has not the past proved as much? Was not the prayer of the great
leader answered (Exod. 33.13)?

8 And as though the thought of Moses triggered a memory, the next chapter of Exodus (34.6) is quoted. It is a most precious thought.

9 As Isaiah 57.16 says, He will not always bear on man with chastisement or man would wither before Him.

10 He is no meticulous weigher-out of penalties.

11 He merely asks for penitence and in the mightiness of His mercy forgives.

12 And He so forgives that no record or memorial is kept, as said Micah in wonder (7.19); so too Isaiah (38.17).

13 God is represented in the psalms as King, as Judge and in other stern roles. It is moving to find Him under the image of a pitying father . . .

14 . . . a pitying father who understands us better than we can ever understand ourselves. 'Does he not know the stuff of which we are made, can he forget that we are only dust?' (Knox).

15 'Poor man! – his days are like the grass, he blooms like a flower in the meadow' (Moffatt).

16 'At the breath of a breeze it is gone and its place never sees it again' (Moffatt). Such thought is common enough in the Old Testament. And how true! The submicroscopic virus, the blockage of an artery, the fluttering of the heart, and the receptacle of a life's learning, the repository of a thousand amazing skills, crumbles. How infinitely horrible were there nothing more, no 'redeeming of life from destruction'.

17 In a word, were there no mercy on such frailty enthroned in the heavens. The psalmist seems but a step from a laying hold of Christian hope.

18 And faithfulness must surely find that mercy.

19 The psalm widens in praise. All is in the hands of a great King – who just before has been a loving Father.

20 That is why the recipient of such mercy can bid the unfallen realms of life to praise God. The redeemed are part of a plan which, according to a curious word of Peter (1 Pet. 1.12), puzzles the angels. 'Maleldil,' says an unfallen creature in one of Lewis' fantasies, 'has done strange things there.'

21 These are the beings which 'carry out His will'. It is left to human beings to pray, 'Thy will be done', a fearful and awesome responsibility when such suppliants hold one portion of the answer in their own care and keeping.

22 And this is why the psalmist returns to his beginning at the end, and bids his soul bless the Lord.

Precisely there is a portion of God's dominion where His writ, if man so desires, does not run. As an old Commentator, J. H. Michaelis, writing in the odd mixture of Latin and Greek proper to the theological writing of his day said: 'The end of this psalm has great pathos. By "epanalepsis" the psalmist returns to his own soul.' The large word, of course, is the figure by which a phrase is repeated after intervening material! Prayer may appropriately both begin and end with ourselves.

Conclusion

> Master, they say that when I seem
> To be in speech with you,
> Since you make no replies, it's all a dream, –
> One talker – aping two.

They are half right, but not as they
Imagine; rather, I
Seek in myself the things I meant to say
And lo! the wells are dry.

Then, seeing me empty, you forsake
The listener's role, and through
My dead lips breathe, and into utterance wake
The thoughts I never knew.

C. S. Lewis. ©

Read Psalm 104

Occasion and author

We cannot know the name of the writer of this beautiful hymn on God in His Creation. Those who stolidly seek for correspondence in literature, have suggested that the writer might have been acquainted with Pharaoh Akhnaton's Hymn to the Sun (see Footnote) written many centuries before the earliest possible date for this magnificent poem. The connection is most unlikely. Sensitive souls, being attuned to the presence of God, seeing the pageantry of created things, can think the same thoughts. They are part of a universal mysticism to be documented from the Egyptian hymn, the Hebrew psalm, to Vergil sensitive to a mighty presence on the wooded, prehistoric Capitol, and to Wordsworth by the Wye above Tintern, sensing 'something far more deeply interfused'. Perhaps the psalm is post-exilic and the writer one who, restored after half a lifetime in the featureless Euphrates plain, saw a land of beauty of which his parents had spoken, a land of hills and streams, and washed by the great sea. Restoration was spiritual as well as geographical and historical. The Jews were close to the earth, a nation of small farmers and shepherds. It was Gentile persecution which drove them to city-dwelling. Nineveh and, supremely, Babylon began the process. For long centuries in Palestine they watched natural things with perceptive eyes, the weather (cf. 65.9–13) dawn and sunset, the great trees, the loveliness of springing water, the manifold living things of jungle and hillside, and even the creatures of the sea, its wide blue circle glimpsed from the high pastures of the land. The beauty and precision of the world, the amazing processes of life, and the machinery of nature reveal God.

Commentary

1–35 The psalms differ as their circumstances and authors differ. Some examine temptation, the emergence and the resolution of an agonizing doubt. Some describe the anatomy of a grief. Some are prayers in which the reader must follow the mind of the writer step by step along some path of thought and seek to understand how some conclusion of hope or climax of faith is reached and held. Hence the difference in modes of study. Some psalms seem carefully constructed and fall into divisions, strophes and themes. Some seem a cry of agony or of jubilation flung on paper. Some, therefore, must be taken phrase by phrase, verse by verse, and the linkage and sequence of thought pondered and examined. Some should be apprehended whole. This psalm, and the two which follow it to complete the book are of that nature.

Read this psalm, therefore, in its completeness. The writer has come to his composition after deep meditation on the Genesis story of the creation and the flood (2,5,6,7), and sees a Presence everywhere interfused. Even the earthquake and the erupting volcano follow some divine command (32), while all creation is bound together, each form of life linked to every other form of life – a fundamental truth which the world is learning amid tribulation. The writer's deep awareness of the integrated pattern of all Creation (27–30) arises from his deep awareness of God. The universe is utterly dependent upon Him (10–24). Everywhere the psalmist sees 'the Word', 'the Vast Intelligence which expressed Itself'. All belief in God can begin thus, as John's Gospel indicates. Subtle philosophies, and a naïve logic which underlies them, seek to 'prove' to some low form of satisfaction, that the old arguments from the existence of the world and its manifest design and purpose (the Cosmological and Teleological Arguments) are not valid, but to most minds which seek a sounder foundation for living, and continuing to live, than Bertrand Russell's 'unyielding despair', agree with the psalmist that the evidence of a Lawgiver is clear in a world reticulated by Law, and that the evidence of a Planner is obvious in a world so intricately purposeful.

Light is His garment (2) and all around, above, beneath are the works of His creating fingers. And it continues. In silence the countless cubic miles of water which form each day's tides rise and fall round the globe (6). The tight cycle of rain and herbage (13,14), the integration of flora and fauna (10–18), the precision of the sun and moon (19,20), and the basic need of man to conform to such precision (23), the perpetually reborn earth (30) so utterly complete until human greed and human sin, the one discordant element, breaks a blessed cycle of renewal – they are all in the psalm. Hence the sudden shock when the lyric suddenly pauses to round on the one corrupter of the vast perfection (35). It is not only where 'the spicy breezes blow over Ceylon's isle', as Bishop Heber put it a trifle unfortunately, that 'every prospect pleases and only man is vile'. A polluted and a damaged planet, hard put to it to regain its health, and as yet far from sure of regaining it, is cause enough for anger against rebel and spoiler.

Footnote

The strangest of all Egypt's Pharaohs came to the throne in 1375 B.C. and lived until 1358 B.C. – a brief life but long enough to encompass an astounding, if frustrated, revolution. Amenhotep IV, or Akhnaton, as he called himself after the Aton he set out to worship, was a noble spirit who sought to break the sombre polytheism and animal totemism of his land, together with the powerful priestly corporations which battened on it. He built a city called 'the Horizon of Aton', which was to be the purged and purified capital of a new Egypt, decorated with the expression of an art based on a newer, nobler theology and a faith in a God who made and sustained all created things. It was an amazing thrust towards monotheism for which Egypt was not ripe. Aton was the sun, an ever-present reality by the Nile, but Aton was not god in the sense in which Egypt had before conceived it, in one facet of her manifold paganism, but only the symbol of an unseen deity's beneficence and care. It was an astonishing leap of faith, but died with its founder when the outraged hierarchy regained ascendancy after the death of the ruler whom they branded as 'the Heretic'. The Pharaoh's charming new capital fell to ruins (and became, in fact, the source of the famous Amarna Letters, part of Akhnaton's Foreign Office files) but enough was left to show that the pure worship of 'the Heretic's' dream begat a love of nature reflected in a new mural art. In the tomb of Ay, father of Akhnaton's queen, Nefertiti, she of the famous Berlin head, a long hymn to the sun has been found. A few verses curiously like parts of the Hebrew hymn may be quoted:

The world is in darkness like the dead . . . Every lion cometh forth from his den; all serpents sting. Darkness reigns.

When Thou risest in the horizon . . . the darkness is banished . . . Then in all the world they do their work.

All trees and plants flourish, . . . the birds flutter in their marshes . . . All sheep dance upon their feet.

The ships sail up-stream and down-stream alike . . . The fish in the river leap up before Thee; and Thy rays are in the midst of the great sea.

How manifold are all Thy works! . . . Thou didst create the earth according to Thy desire, – men, all cattle, . . . all that are upon the earth . . .

Thou hast set a Nile in heaven that it may fall for them, making floods upon the mountains . . . and watering their fields. The Nile in heaven is for the service of the strangers, and for the cattle of every land.

Thou makest the seasons . . . Thou hast made the distant heaven in order to rise therein, . . . dawning, shining afar off, and returning.

The world is in Thy hand, even as Thou hast made them. When Thou hast risen they live; when Thou settest they die . . . By Thee man liveth.

105

Read Psalm 105; 1 Chronicles 16.8-22

Occasion and author

This is fairly clearly a poem of the same group, from the same writer or school of writers from which the preceding psalm came. It follows as does the next psalm logically enough, the theme of Psalm One Hundred and Four. God has been hymned as a glorious Creator, visible to the eye of faith in the beauty, the order, and the coherence of His wonderful world. Like the writer of Psa. 78, the author now turns to history, in the outworking of which the eye of faith can again discern an immense and mighty presence, a moral law outworking, which speaks of a vast observing mind. History is traversed as a theme for thankfulness and a study which prompts a trustful obedience.

Commentary

1–15 These verses appear in the Chronicler's story (1 Chron. 16.8–22) as part of the festal song which accompanied the ark to Zion. If this psalm is, as one might surmise, a psalm of the Restoration, or even of the quieter closing days of the exile, then the later writer must have incorporated the earlier poem. It is of small consequence. The theme of God's faithfulness in keeping His covenant is pursued with jubilation (1–3), confident faith (4) and deep awareness of God's promises. The theme is Hebraic and, in consequence, less moving to the Christian reader, save that a covenant, as the Old Testament conceived it, was a foreshadowing of grace. A covenant initiated with God, a binding promise, a free gift of love.

16–25 History was interpreted in the light of this. Disaster, as man conceived it, pain, suffering, were not precluded by the covenant. How else explain the catastrophes endured by a favoured people, unless it followed that suffering was significant, pain designed to teach, to purify, to punish? Egypt is dealt with at length as though that captivity in some way mirrored the Babylonian exile. And Egypt's experience, indeed, had its purpose. Joseph's sufferings were themselves vicarious. He was sent ahead to prepare the way for Israel's dwelling in Egypt, and from that experience they emerged a nation.

26–38 If the preceding psalm grew out of long and fruitful meditations on Genesis, this psalm reflects a similar pondering over the second book of the Pentateuch, the story of Moses, greatest of national saviours, and the dire disasters which fell on those who misused the people of the covenant. Observe that leaders are not glorified. There is no ode in honour of Moses. The glory of the nation forms no theme. When the nation is prominent, as in the next psalm, it is in a context of rebuke. It is 'God who is given the glory' – a fact unique in the patriotic literature of nations.

39–45 The writer takes the story through to Canaan's peace. Perhaps, in the psalm, is an interesting glimpse of a habit of the exile. It has been pointed out before in these studies, and there will be occasion to stress the fact in later psalms, that the exile forced the people to revere the Word. It is not unlikely that the knowledge of vital history was kept alive and transmitted by methods common enough in the early days of a people's history. Ballad and epic arise from the desire to enshrine significant story in song, and such poems as this may be relics of the songs of exile.

Footnote

Verse 18 contains in Coverdale's Prayer Book Version one of those mistranslations we should not willingly lose. 'The iron entered into his soul', has become a metaphor in English for the hardness which suffering can bring – the last thing that was true of Joseph. The Hebrew says literally 'his soul came into iron' and 'his soul' means simply 'he' – cf. 94.17. The Syriac, Septuagint and Jerome's Latin follow the Hebrew quite literally.

Coverdale seems to have followed a later edition of the Vulgate which read 'ferrum transiit animam eius' – 'the iron went into his soul'. The RSV is perverse. *Nephesh*, the Hebrew for 'soul', is commonly used for the person to avoid a pronoun.

Conclusion

As with a people, so with the individual. We do well not to forget our own story, to look back habitually in praise and with enlivened understanding at the path we have trod, and to become aware with the tuition of the years of the reality of the Guiding Hand.

With mercy and with judgement,
My web of time He wove,
And aye the dews of sorrow
Were lustred by His Love;
I'll bless the hand that guided,
I'll bless the heart that planned,
When throned where glory dwelleth
In Immanuel's land.

I've wrestled on towards heaven,
'Gainst storm, and wind, and tide;
Now like a weary trav'ller
That leaneth on his guide.
Amid the shades of ev'ning,
While sinks life's lingering sand,
I hail the glory dawning
In Immanuel's land.

106

Read Psalm 106; Daniel 9

Occasion and author

The writer is surely the poet who wrote the preceding psalm. He is closing the book, and penitence is an appropriate theme. 'Of all the acts of man,' said Carlyle, 'repentance is the most divine. The greatest of all faults is to be conscious of none'. And Jeremy Taylor: 'It is the greatest and dearest blessing that ever God gave to men that they may repent; and therefore to deny it or delay it is to refuse health when brought by the skill of the physician – to refuse liberty offered to us by our gracious Lord.' The occasion must have been a time of chastening, perhaps, again, as the exile of the people was manifestly drawing to an end but was not yet complete (47). It is obvious enough that the great repatriation must have been a matter of years and an operation more complicated than either Ezra or Nehemiah shows.

Commentary

1–5 The psalm is an utterance of some formality. The writer approaches God with reverent feet, thinks of His goodness (1), His love (1), His care (2), His demand for justice and righteousness (4), and the reality of His covenant. He picks up the theme of the last psalm.

6,7 This psalm, in fact complements the one which precedes it. Confession naturally follows the review of God's goodness in history. 'The confession of evil works,' said Augustine rightly, 'is the first beginning of good works.' 'Surely never but in Israel,' writes Maclaren, 'has patriotism chosen the nation's sins as the theme of song . . . in the Psalter we have several hymns of national confession.' And see Deuteronomy 26, 1 Kings 8, Nehemiah 9 and Daniel 9.

8–42 Then, as though driven by some sense of duty, the singer of God's goodness traverses conscientiously the story of the preceding psalm, and ruthlessly exposes the human response to the tale of deliverance and emerging nationhood which he has told. Into this long catalogue of reluctance, hesitant discipleship, and tardy following, we can hardly enter. It is a national confession. As a nation, as individuals, we each have similar confessions to make. The ancient record of shame over idolatry, disobedience, faithlessness and compromise, can be a pattern for any other people swept by some gust of self-realization. It can be a framework for our own unworthiness. But we do seem to be listening to another's self-abasement and can scarcely say more than: 'There, but for God's rich grace, goes my people, there, in truth go I.'

Observe v. 15. It is a factor in the theme of 'unaswered prayer'. Juvenal, the Roman satirist, said, 'the gods have overturned whole houses in answer to their masters' prayers.' Midas prayed that all he touched should turn to gold. It did! Tithonus, in the myth, prayed for immortality, but forgot to pray for immortal youth. 'Ignorant of ourselves,' says Menecrates to Pompey in *Antony and Cleopatra*, 'we beg often our own harms', and 'find profit in the losing of our prayers'. 'Thy will be done' should accompany all prayer. Israel asked in sin, and judgement came.

43–46 Having steeled himself to reveal all, and put the whole story without self-pity into uncompromising words, the psalmist turns with relief to the loving kindness which has heard, delivered, remembered, pitied and healed. The covenant, forgotten by men, misconceived, abused, is none the less remembered by the One who made it. His love, as the opening verses said, endures for ever. Failure is not final. There is always a tomorrow. Forgiveness is absolute and inexhaustible. It still awaits a world's, a nation's repentance. And was there ever time when our own nation needed more to grasp that fact, to remember a vast heritage, mercy and deliverance given . . .?

47,48 The storm dies. The clouds roll from a troubled sky. The sun comes out with healing in its wings. The book ends with a doxology in which we can, with whole heart, join.

Conclusion

Let the conclusion be a famous hymn:

> *Rock of Ages, cleft for me,*
> *Let me hide myself in Thee;*
> *Let the water and the blood,*
> *From Thy riven side which flowed*
> *Be of sin the double cure —*
> *Cleanse me from its guilt and pow'r.*

> *Nothing in my hand I bring,*
> *Simply to Thy Cross I cling;*
> *Naked, come to Thee for dress;*
> *Helpless, look to Thee for grace;*
> *Foul, I to the fountain fly;*
> *Wash me, Saviour, or I die.*

INTRODUCTION TO BOOK FIVE

A shadowy figure has haunted these studies on the Psalms – the unknown scholar, if indeed there was only one, who put the Psalter in order. In Book Five we seem close upon his trail. No account, of course, is extant on how the Psalter was put together. There is some suggestion that it was originally three books, and was expanded into five to match the Pentateuch. In the present form it goes back at least to three centuries before Christ, on the evidence of the Septuagint.

In Book Five the compiler, editor, or whatever we choose to call him had a varied mass of material to put in order. He clearly had some existing smaller collections. There was a group of 'hallelujah psalms', perhaps from the music-masters of the Second Temple and designed for the worship of the shrine. To avoid monotony these were divided and placed near the beginning and near the end of the book.

Next there were the two 'Hallels' – the so-called 'Egyptian Hallel' (113–118) and the 'Great Hallel' (120–136). This group, or at least the greater part of it (120–134), was also called 'the Songs of Ascent', a term of some looseness of definition. He had also the longest of all the Psalms (119), itself a minor collection of sayings about the Word. This was placed firmly in the middle of the book, perhaps for artistic reasons, though convenience in the actual handling of a papyrus roll, and moving the weight from stick to stick is not an irrelevant consideration.

To vary the collection the compiler also found available some psalms of David, largely psalms of personal experience which had not found a place in earlier tracts of traditionally Davidic poems. There were also similar psalms (for example 110, 130 and 137), anonymous but of like nature. It is obvious that this mass of material was handled well with a perceptive eye to balance and variety. He had also the simple duty of preserving a certain length.The papyrus roll had its limits. That is why Pss. 106 and 107 are separated, though obviously from the same hand. One concludes Book Four, the other opens Book Five.

If conjecture could be permitted to stray a little further, it might be imagined that the collector of good words who was responsible for putting Psa. 119 together (was he a scholar who had experienced the Exile?) also edited the Psalter, and wrote Psalm One, last of all, to make a choice intro-duction. But to put forward such an unprovable suggestion with anything other than the lightest of hands would be to stray into the embarrassing company of those who profess to know how the Pentateuch precariously grew. And anyone familiar with literary criticism as scholarship applies it in any other sphere of ancient writing, would shun such fellowship.

Occasion and author

The author of this vivid and confident psalm is unknown, but it is surely the same poet as he who wrote the preceding three psalms. They seem to form a tetralogy and the break in sequence by the arbitrary division of the Fifth Book from the Fourth breaks a chain of thought. The time would seem to be after a wide ingathering from the Dispersion, not only from their northern exile but from other quarters also. This is perhaps an indication that a considerable exodus of refugees had escaped the Babylonian deportation. There is, of course, some evidence of this in Jeremiah's story. It is a time of rejoicing and the psalmist's mind is overwhelmed by the thought of God's deliverance, the thought that a moral law does, after all, operate in history, and that a great vindication of sorely tried faith had taken place.

Commentary

1–3 Gratitude is the theme. Verse 3 answers 106.41. The time has come. God has shown His hand. The promises, long delayed, have come to fulfilment. It was an hour in which it was good to be alive. The land, long depopulated, was filling again. There are echoes of Isaiah (43.5,6; 62.12; 63.4).

4–9 The sudden description of the lost caravan may be autobiographical, or allude to some experience of near-disaster and deliverance within the knowledge of the writer. It could have happened to some band of refugees. The roads were full of them when Nebuchadnezzar rolled down on Jerusalem – a tragic sight with which this war-ridden century is too familiar. It could refer to a lost band of returning exiles. The desert roads could be the occasion of such catastrophe. It could refer metaphorically to the fate of the nation, uprooted, driven into the wilderness, lost. Against this interpretation is the vivid literalness of the later description of the tempest-tossed sailor. The writer snatches a scene from life, desperation, deliverance, and calls for due adoration to One who can save. That God sometimes does not intervene in the manner in which the psalmist seems to imply that He invariably will, is a question to be faced in the concluding remarks.

10–16 Having seen national disaster and restoration the psalmist is eloquent over the moral law, and the principles of judgement which he sees interwoven with the fabric of human history. This was a theme in the thinking of the Old Testament prophets, and in stressing it they anticipated Herodotus, Toynbee and others who have sought for some moral or spiritual law in history. Herodotus pondered on the question of why the mighty empire of Persia was unable to crush the little, divided land of Greece. Toynbee, dissecting a score of human cultures in his row of massive volumes, discovered a pattern of rise and fall bound together with an invariable principle of coherence and disintegration. Herbert Butterfield, one time Professor of History at Cambridge, has an eloquent chapter on 'Judgement in History' in his fine book of 1947, *Christianity and History*. Christians should study such themes. The verses in this section are a statement of the writer's confidence that the mills of God are grinding. That they grind so slowly, sometimes, is a problem which torments other psalmists, but is there any hymnbook, which does not contain hymns, true enough in the writer's experience, true even in general, but which make sad and stumbling singing for some who, on a narrower plane of life, have found much to distress them?

17–22 If the line is taken that this psalm is a series of metaphors for the people's exile and return, this passage likens the whole hurtful tract of trouble to a self-inflicted illness, from which God's healing hand, in response to penitence and prayer, brought recovery to health. Again the theme, literal or metaphorical, about a person or about people, pursues only one simple line. This is how it can happen. There are however, illnesses which are not the fruit of folly or sin, which are not God's judgement, and which do not end in recovery. In the euphoria of the hour, the psalmist is not facing these heavy problems. It was, for him, a dawn of confidence, and in life's variety such days come.

23–32 The Phoenicians to the north were great shipmen. The Hebrews were landsmen with a long harbourless coast, and they had some horror of the sea. The description of a storm will be appreciated by anyone who has not the gift of invulnerability on an unsteady, lurching deck. But for all the vividness of the description, there is still nothing to forbid the interpretation that this is again a picture of the troubled nation. 'The Ship of State' is common enough metaphor. Centuries later, in 38 B.C. when civil war was still a reality in the Roman world, Horace, the poet, put the thought into an elaborate allegory:

> *Ship of the State beware!*
> *Hold fast the port. Cling to the friendly shore;*
> *Lest sudden storms, and whirling eddies bear*
> *Thy shattered hull to faithless seas once more.*

> *See how the rower faints upon his oar!*
> *Hark to the groaning of the mast*
> *Sore stricken by the Libyan blast!*
> *Thy shrouds are burst; thy sails are torn;*
> *And through thy gaping ribs forlorn*
> *The floods remorseless pour.*

> *Dare not to call for aid on powers divine;*
> *Dishonoured once they hear no more;*
> *Nor boast, majestic pine,*
> *Daughter of Pontic forests, thy great name,*
> *Old lineage, well-earned fame,*

The honours of thy sculptured prow:
Sport of the mocking winds, nor feared, nor trusted now!
Alas my country, long my anxious care,
Source now of bitter pain, and fond regret!
Thy stars obscured, thy course beset
By rocks unseen, beware!
Trust not soft winds and treacherous seas
Or the false glitter of the Cyclades.

(*Odes* 1,14. S. E. De Vere's rather heavy rendering).

Longfellow, assuredly with the Latin poem in mind, similarly addressed the Ship of State:

Thou, too, sail on thou Ship of State!
Sail on, O Union, strong and great!
Humanity with all its fears,
With all its hopes of future years,
Is hanging breathless on thy fate.

Again, his nation's ship in harbour, the psalmist passes over the associated problems. Calvin, seeing a church full of votive offerings from those rescued from storm and sea, remarked, 'I see no record of those who perished'.

33–43 The concluding eleven verses break the pattern of the psalm but are not incongruous with it. The evil and the worth of man can both find reflection in the landscape. In this age of environmental menace, the world is too well aware of man-made deserts. The land of Babylon which the exiles had lately known, lush, irrigated, full of fruitfulness, was itself to become a salty waste. On the other hand, any visitor to Israel can see the deserts coming into usefulness and greening under the industrious and inventive hands of man.

The theme of thankfulness is still implicit though not so directly expressed in this closing movement of the psalm. Man takes the movement of the seasons and the productivity of the earth too easily for granted. The shift of rain belts in some periodic desiccation of the Sahara, the genesis of Mediterranean weather, may have destroyed the early Mycenaean civilization of Greece. The Sahara again threatens African history.

In Psa. 65 we saw the psalmist turn to the wonder of the world around him, the might of the hills and the troubled surging of the sea which sinks to rest under the touch of God's finger, just as the turmoil of the nations dies under His word.

The wonder of the rain now commands attention and the health-giving beauty of water, blessings more vividly appreciated in lands of abundant rainfall. In a favoured world, a well-fed minority and an affluent society fail at times to appreciate the wonder of the harvest, and life's dependence on its recurring miracle.

Efficient farming, good communications, scientific storage, and packaged food make an easy-going world forget that it all depends upon the gift of Heaven's rain, and God's devising. The sheep-studded hills and the billowing corn are the gift of His grace, and should be counted among the multitude of His tender mercies.

Conclusion

The problem of this psalm has been touched upon already in passing. It is one which the troubled Christian meets again and again, faced by too facile preaching, hearing in story and 'testimony' the carefully tailored experience of the more fortunate, the less anxious, the simpler souls of this world. Recapitulate. The writer of this psalm at a high tide of fulfilment and obviously answered prayer calls the recipients of God's blessings to gratitude. He says no more. He is describing situations in life and in history which are real, deliverances which have taken place. He likens a tract of his nation's history to all of these cameos of circumstance. Let us read the psalm within the narrow compass of this purpose. Other psalms have been far from such confidence. We have seen the travail of soul of good men. We can turn to Job and to Habakkuk and see ourselves in days of harder trails. These are other facets of life. The Christian has Calvary to contemplate. *He* was betrayed, the Christ of God; *He* met injustice, sorrow and acquaintance with grief; *He* was murdered – and out of it came the way of God's salvation. In Christ God bids us wait, suffer if need be with Christ, and trust that out of all such tribulation good will come in so far as the whole has been surrendered to His creative hands. The nation caught at the moment of this psalm has been through the fire, is comforted, her warfare accomplished. Who shall grudge this shout of jubilation?

Read Psalms 57; 60; 108

This psalm is a conflation of parts of two earlier psalms: 57.7–11 and 60.5–12. There are unimportant modifications of language. Since praise is a dominant note in the psalms of Book Five, it is not impossible that this adaptation of two Davidic psalms provided the editor with a piece that he thought proper to include, or, alternatively, provided someone else with a triumph song which assumed an identity in its own right. Comments will be found in the commentaries on the earlier psalms.

76

109

Read Psalm 109

Occasion and author

The identity of the object of the denunciations of this psalm, be it Shimei, Doeg or any other traitor, is not important. The ancient heading ascribes the imprecation to David, and the words can here and there be paralleled in earlier psalms. The puzzle is why a psalm so fierce in its call for retribution should have been placed precisely here in the Psalter. It intrudes into a group of psalms notable for their mood of praise and thankfulness.

It is difficult to find a satisfying explanation within the context of a true respect for the authority of Scripture. Peter (Acts 1.20) briefly quotes, and the psalm has been called the 'Judas Psalm'. But who, even on that night of vast betrayal, would have spoken thus to Judas? The consequences of his deed needed no words.

Calvin contradicts himself. He is clearly shocked by the violence but suggests that David was not speaking from a fount of personal resentment, nor pursuing a private hatred or vendetta. He was merely a vehicle for the denunciation of the unrighteous. Christ, he stressed, set us the example: 'You know not of what spirit you are.' And Calvin proceeds to denounce the practice of hiring compliant friars to pronounce these words of woe against specific individuals.

Suffering can sometimes tempt the hurt and the persecuted to immoderation of speech. At the end of Tertullian's *De Spectaculis* there is a horrifying passage in which that fiery churchman relishes the prospect of the glee with which he hoped to watch, writhing in judgement-fire, persecutor and philosopher, tyrant and actor – all, in short, who had opposed Christ or ministered to the flesh.

This is not, of course, solving the problem of the imprecatory psalms. In Psa. 137, another of the psalms which disturb the Christian reader, a fairly good reason for the outburst of cursing can be advanced. It hardly applies here. But let us proceed constructively . . . Let us remember first of all that, not only in the New Testament, but also in the Old the spirit of vindictiveness is deprecated. Look at Lev. 19.17,18; 'You shall not hate your brother in your heart . . . nor avenge nor bear any grudge against the children of your people. You shall love your neighbour as yourself.' And in Exod. 23.4,5: 'If you meet your enemy's ox or ass going astray you shall bring it back to him. If you see the ass of one who hates you lying under his burden . . . you must help him.' It is the same in Proverbs: 'Do not rejoice when your enemy falls nor let your heart be glad when he stumbles.' A verse from the next chapter

77

is quoted by Paul: 'If your enemy hunger, give him food' (Prov. 24.17; 25.21). All this is far removed from the imprecations of Psalm 109.

First, as was remarked earlier in these studies about the wild protestations and complaints which haunt some of the psalms, it is better to have out before God what is inside. C. S. Lewis attempted in his not wholly satisfactory chapter on this problem, to set the 'cursings' in historical context, and that thought is important. 'These poets,' he wrote, 'lived in a world of savage punishments, of massacre and violence . . .' They did, and such horrors are not yet banished from the world. And perhaps with this thought we are drawing a little closer to the reason why the one who put these psalms in order placed this poem of imprecation where he did. A whole people had been dragged across the desert roads to Babylon. Every mile must have seen the old, the weak, the injured, the sick, the young and helpless, fall and die. The whip, the club, the spear drove them on. In Babylon they were slaves, cursed, derided, tortured, killed by toil and by cruelty. Only those who have suffered thus can feel free to comment on what seethed in their crushed, tormented spirits, and sprang in blazing words to their praying lips. Perhaps this psalm is placed here deliberately and without comment to illustrate, after the frank manner of the Bible, what fiendish men had done to the minds and hearts of their foes. As Lewis continues: 'We must think of those who made them so. These hatreds are the reaction to something . . . the kind of thing that cruelty and injustice by a sort of natural law, produce.' If we believe, as we must surely believe, that divine overruling guided the 'holy men of old' who determined the canon of Scripture, then such a psalm is placed thus as a demonstration, a comment on Babylon and what Babylon did, not a form of words to be followed.

It is an awful and solemnizing thought, too, that the precise judgement called for in the psalm fell on the Babylonian empire. The cruel imperialists had fought against Israel without cause (3), they had requited evil for good (5). And wicked men of their own pattern were to rule them (6), the mad Cambyses, the vile Ahasuerus. Such men 'took the office' (8) of Nebuchadnezzar and Belshazzar. Their mighty city is still a ruin waste (10). They were cruel, persecutors, murderers of the humble (16), men of foul mouths (17-19) – and they were conquered as they had conquered, brought down as they had brought down, enslaved as they had enslaved. Verse 18 is a terrible picture of dedicated and utter evil. Like a robe or a girdle (19) it enfolds the man; like water drunk it passes deep within him and circulates in his blood; like oil it penetrates every crevice of the soul.

Commentary

Much of what can, or needs, to be said about this sombre psalm, especially up to v. 20, is in the introductory remarks. At the next verse the writer turns from his enemies, personified in the person of their king, to God, and the psalm moves into the imagery of pain and sorrow which is not uncommon in the Psalter. Part of the urgency for vindication and the visible operation of God's retribution and judgement upon sin, is that his days are few (23) and he is shamed before triumphant evil (25). God has promised otherwise (26), so why must He delay (27)?

110

Read Psalm 110; Hebrews 5; 7

Occasion and author

To accept the tradition that this psalm, quoted beyond all others in the New Testament, is a 'psalm of David', by no means precludes the thought that it might be an utterance of David's priest and mentor, the brave Nathan (see 2 Sam. 7). It is a 'Messianic psalm', on the Lord's own authority (Matt. 22.41–45; Mark 12.35–37), and by 'Messianic' is meant that flashes of insight into a future yet unknown, and a royal visitant yet to be, are intermingled with the text. There seems to have been no primary meaning, no special occasion in David's life of such nature that it could absorb the original significance of the psalm. It is a mysterious utterance which seems to pierce through the veil of time and symbolically speak of the triumph of Christ – a species of apocalypse.

Commentary

1–4 To sit at one's right hand implied a distinctive honour (Psa. 45.9; 1 Kings 2.19). See also Acts 2.34–36, Eph. 1.20–22 and Heb. 1.13,14 for the authority which, in this context, accompanies the designation of honour. Archaeology illustrates the metaphor of the footstool. A footstool from Tutankhamen's tomb is decorated with figures of Semites and Nubians, types of Pharaoh's enemies. See too Josh. 10.24,25.

The Kingdom of Christ is the figure used in Messianic poetry to signify the ultimate triumph of the Lord. It is reminiscent of the language of the Apocalypse in which the metaphors of royal authority are used to speak of the ultimate consummation of God's purposes in Christ. It is always to be remembered that the Lord's first followers misconceived 'the Kingdom'. Whatever its incomprehensible shape and fashion will be, it will transcend anything which can be imagined about it.

On v. 4 the best commentary is, of course Heb. 5 and 7. Melchizedek, King of Salem, is a mysterious person. No parents are mentioned, no descendants, and yet he was a person of such royal and priestly dignity that Abraham, already a chieftain of standing and the conscious bearer of God's promises, bowed before his majesty and gave him tribute. He is regarded here, and the theme is developed by the writer to the Hebrews, as a pre-figuring of Christ.

Verse 4 looks forward to one who combines the offices of king (1,2,3) and priest (4), but a priest of no common order, more ancient than the priest-hood of Aaron. The argument is developed cogently in the epistle, and may

79

be left to tell its own story. It was a priesthood antedating the law. It was a Gentile priesthood, two points of extreme significance in a letter to Jewish Christians uneasy over the passing of Judaism into a global faith.

5-7 The theme moves to the day of judgement on evil, still in the imagery of a royal conqueror. The image of the refreshing stream in v. 7 is difficult to interpret. No commentator has a satisfactory explanation, and no translation has been legitimately adjusted to make a true sequence of sense. It must be left as it is. Perhaps there is some very ancient damage to the text.

Conclusion
It is already written: 'And I saw heaven opened, and look, a white horse. And He who sat upon it was called Faithful and True and it is in righteousness that He judges and makes war. His eyes were like a flame of fire and on His head were many crowns and He had a name written which none knew but He. He was clothed with a garment dipped in blood and His name is *The Word of God.*'

111, 112

Read Psalms 111; 112

Occasion and author
These two hymns were probably from the pen of one of the Temple musicians – a man skilled in the writing of highly formal verse. In most literatures, especially in post-classical times, the cult of artificial poetry arises. It is often, for all the artificiality, fine verse and inspiration can find its way through all forms of literature. The sonnet, in modern European literature was the only form of such verse to attain a front place in literature. In Hebrew the art took the form of alphabetical word play. These two poems, which obviously go together, are striking examples. The skills of men are as varied as those who practise them. Given to God, all forms of human communication can find their usefulness.

In this bracket of two psalms, the letters of the Hebrew alphabet not only mark the beginning of the first word in each verse, but the beginning of each clause within the verses. In both psalms there are twenty-two lines corresponding to the letters in the Hebrew alphabet. The first eight verses in each psalm consist of two lines, and the last two verses of three. The two psalms correspond in thought as well as in structure. The same phrases recur. In the first the deeds, the glory, and the righteousness of God are celebrated in the congregation of the good. In the second psalm the righteousness, the worth and the happiness of the good themselves are celebrated.

Commentary

111. 1–4   The two psalms are 'hallelujah psalms', and thus placed because of their obvious association with the two 'Hallels' which are incorporated into Book Five. The 'hallelujah' with which the psalm opens stands outside the acrostic order.

Praise is to rise from the depths of the whole person (the 'heart'), something more than what Bunyan called 'a lick of the tongue'. 'The works of the Lord', what Paul calls 'the multitude of His tender mercies' are the motive, and the verse stresses the need 'to study' them. This is a theme for meditation on varied levels of life, historical, personal. God's goodness towards us is often so interwoven with the texture of circumstance that we fail to see the subtle planning of His mind and the movement of His hand. Hence the need to pause, to look, to think. He does what He does in a manner 'to be remembered' (4, KJV). We are too forgetful and fail too often to tap a deep spring of faith, of hope, of courage to go on.

5–10   'Holy and awesome is His name' (9, NASB). The writer alludes covertly to the majestic history of the race, a purposeful plan, newly vindicated in the experience of restoration to the land. The greatest irreverence towards God, as Ruskin once remarked, is to banish Him from our thoughts. To ponder the movements of ultimate love and wisdom in the pattern of our days, cannot but produce that quiet wonder which is the soul of awe. Reverence is an ennobling sentiment. Only the fool can treat sacred, beautiful and majestic things with inconsequence and flippancy. Hence v. 10. Wisdom's chief ingredient is reverence. Reverence is also the foundation of virtue. To treat the body and the mind as realities of surpassing wonder, is to halt short of abusing them. To treat the great virtues with reverence is to safeguard them. Tennyson, who saw deeply into the things of the spirit, put it well in his prologue to *In Memoriam*:

> *Let knowledge grow from more to more,*
> *But more of reverence in us dwell;*
> *That mind and soul, according well,*
> *May make one music as before,*
> *But vaster.*

112. 1–3   Now comes, to borrow the terminology of the choric songs of Greek drama, the antistrophe. After the call to praise, the beatitude follows. 'Happy is he who holds God in reverence.' The 'fear of God' contains nothing base, degrading, dehumanizing. It delivers from the fear of man. There is a virtuous fear and a vicious fear, as Pascal pointed out. 'Persons of the one character fear to lose God; those of the other character fear to find Him.'

The thought in the writer's mind is that the maintenance of Israel's new-found life is in a holy reverence for the God who had saved them (2).

4,5   The compassion of God finds its way through and out from the personalities of righteous men. Society is sick, and the world diseased with violence, selfishness, cruelty and uncleanness because there are too few upright men, men and women of reverence for God, and the goodness which springs from that association.

6–8 Nations still bent and bowing under the weight of their problems could regain health, vigour and happiness if by some miracle of sweeping revival the army of the good could stand up again, unshaken (6), unafraid (7,8), firm, faithful (8).

9,10 There is nothing vicious in satisfaction over the discomfiture of the vicious, even in rejoicing over the defeat of evil. Homer, with a similar thought in mind, remarks on the beauty of the home where a man and a woman live in love to the joy of their friends, and the discomfort of their enemies. Pity is wasted on evil.

113

Read Psalm 113; Matthew 26.20–30

Occasion and author

This hymn of praise is the first of the psalms comprising the Hallel, which was sung at the three great feasts, Passover, Pentecost, and Tabernacles. The group of six psalms, beginning, said tradition, with a song of Moses, was called, from the opening verse of the next psalm, 'the Egyptian Hallel'. Pss. 113 and 114 were sung before the Passover meal, and Pss. 115–118 after it. Hence the hymn they sang at the Last Supper. The group of psalms should be read in the light of this event.

Commentary

1–3 The 'name of the Lord' in the ancient concept meant the Lord and all that word signified. Praise is reverence and, in a context of prayer, involves quiet thought of Him whom we approach. It is, as v. 3 implies, an attitude of the mind and heart rather than a formal utterance. It is thus that we 'pray without ceasing'.

4–6 John's Gospel embraces a similar sweep of thought. 'In the beginning was a Mind which expressed itself. That Mind was God and created everything that was made . . . That Mind, that Vast Intelligence, became a human being and dwelt for a time among us. So we learned what God really was and what grace was too . . .'

It is appropriate that v. 6 should glimpse afar the Incarnation. In Christ is seen the ultimate self-humbling of God. He 'made Himself of no reputation, and took upon Him the form of a servant, and was made in the likeness of men, and being found in fashion as a man, He humbled Himself, and became obedient unto death, even the death of the cross.' It overwhelms the soul to think that the Lord had all this in mind as He sang the Hallel on the betrayal night. Maclaren comments on this psalm, 'Exultant and world-filling should be the praises from the lips of those who know how low He has stooped and how high He has risen, and how surely all who hold His hand will be lifted from any ash-heap and set on His throne, sharers in the royalty of Him who has been partaker of their weakness.'

7-9 Hannah used vs. 7 and 8, an indication, perhaps, of the venerable antiquity of this hymn of praise.

Read Psalm 114; Joshua 3.14–17

Occasion and author

This compact and beautifully constructed psalm is a lyric poem of praise. The author can hardly have been Moses, for events extend into the days of Joshua's leadership. The people were back from Babylon, captivity, and exile in a land of strange speech. It was natural that thought should turn back to the Exodus, the great deliverance in which their nation had been born. God had gone before them with power, and nature itself had been the tool of His salvation. The return from exile was like a second Exodus, and the returning Jews found joy and confidence in the contemplation of the past. Such is the use of both history and experience. The soul is fortified by the contemplation of what God has done in time past and can do again to deliver and to save.

Commentary

1,2 The psalm is divided into strophes of two verses. 'A strange language', with its barrier to communication, is a force which alienates, inspires loneliness and sometimes fear. Exod. 15.17 calls the land a sanctuary and Exod. 19.6 the people God's priests. Verse 2 conflates the ideas. They travelled with the Tent of Witness in the midst, the symbol of God's invisible presence, His guidance and His care.

3,4 The curious reference to the plunging hills may enshrine a recollection which does not appear in the historical account of the crossing of Jordan. The crossing of the river appears to have taken place at Adam, the modern Tell Damiyeh, some 16 miles north of Jericho. At this point in the valley the banks are high and unstable in structure and easily undermined by flood-waters. The Jordan was, in fact, running high at the time. The Rift Valley was seismically unstable at the time, and earthquakes have frequently dammed the stream by flinging large landslides across the bed. In A.D. 1267 such a dam blocked the river for 16 hours. In 1906 a similar event occurred, and in 1927 the waters were piled up and 'driven back' for over 21 hours. Such was probably the machinery of the miracle.

5,6 This striking apostrophe is effective. The poet sees the event as though

83

it was taking place. The great sandbanks and glistening mud appear as the Red Sea draws back, the trench of the river empties. The hills which had heaved dizzily grow still . . .

7,8 And the reason? The shadow of God's hand has passed over the scene. So it was on Galilee – mad tumult and then great calm. So, thank God, it can be at times in life.

115

Read Psalm 115; Nehemiah 2

Occasion and author
This psalm appears again to come from the days of the restoration. The early chapters of Nehemiah provide the background. In deep devotion, holding hard to the faith that God had brought them home, the exiles faced the desolation and the ruin of their land, fought to suppress the thought o the vast and beautiful city which pagans had built for themselves, and set out in stress and toil to reconstruct Jerusalem.

Commentary
1–8 Scoffing foes surrounded them as they struggled with the tumbled stone, and courage could be maintained only while the heart was fixed and the mind stayed on Almighty God. In Babylon the exiles had learned to look with scorn and contempt on the carved objects of heathen worship. Verse 8 is the result of observation. They had seen human beings create gods in their own image, deities of lust and cruelty, malicious and base as those who made them. They had seen the corrupt worship of such gods react on the worshipper and establish in life and conduct the vicious qualities imagined in the deity. People become like the objects of their worship. That is why it is so important to see God as He would have us see Him, in the form and lineaments of Jesus Christ. 'The only begotten Son, He has revealed Him', says John 1.18, and contemplation of that Person fills the mind with the true image of God, and builds into the character the love and mercy, the purity and righteousness which are the Lord's. Unto His name as the psalm says, be all the glory.

9–11 The congregation, it might be supposed, sing in unison the first eight verses. Verses 9–11 are taken up, perhaps with some change in the music, by the Levitical choir.

12–15 It has also been conjectured that the priest alone intoned this benediction and that v. 12 marks the precise moment of the sacrifice.

16–18 It would follow, if this conjectural division is correct, that the congregation took up the theme again, and closed the time of worship with this passage.

116

Occasion and author

The author of this sincere and moving little poem of thanks is unknown. It reads like many of the earlier psalms of David. It is not clear why it was placed here in the Psalter unless it was to break the continuity of the 'hallelujah psalms'. Many reasons beyond all conjecture could determine such matters. For example, the compiler or editor of Book Five could have thus placed his personal signature in the form of a psalm struck from an experience of the moment, some sickness or peril of life interrupting his vital work . . .

Obviously danger had been real and dire (3,9,15), and the response shows the reality and depth of personal faith and devotion of a Jew of the Restoration, a faith deepened and widened perhaps in the stress and pain of the Exile itself. Phrases from earlier psalms intrude, but these psalms held in the memory and passed from one to another through the long years had been part of the bond which had held the nation, its faith and its hope together in the long captivity.

Commentary

1 'I love' has no object actually expressed. It is obviously God, but it is as though the writer simply wanted to think of the all-enveloping emotion. It could be a feature of his style. 'Call' in the next verse has no object expressed, obvious though it is to whom the cry goes out. Augustine commented on this verse in elegant Latin: 'Let the soul which wanders from the Lord sing this; let the sheep which had strayed sing this; let the son who was dead and had come back to life sing this, he who had perished and is found; let our soul sing this, brothers and sons most beloved.'

2 The beautiful picture of one stopping to attend and listen is too often erased in more prosaic modern versions. It should be kept as in the KJV. The King has paused to hear His humble suppliant, and confidence in His royal care will live as long as life.

3 Echoes, of course, of a psalm of David (18.1–6), but why not? As with many a Scottish congregation, the psalms were part of the pattern of thinking and of speech. 'Death's noose about me, caught in the snares of the grave, ever I found distress and grief at my side' (Knox). He was caught by the two grim huntsmen, and they closed in round his very bed.

4 'Save my life' (RSV) is probably the better rendering in the Old Testament context. A brief prayer, but need prayers be long? The Lord said as

85

much: 'They think that they will be heard because of their much-speaking' (Matt. 6.7).

5 Delicately, he speaks of those attributes of God which brought the answer. Answered prayer has instructed the suppliant in the knowledge of God's very nature. Kindness, goodness, mercy are the thoughts which fill the writer's mind and load the verse with meaning.

6 'Simple' is used in the proverbs for the culpably ignorant. Here it means the humble as the antiphonal part of the verse signifies. Humility is an active virtue, truly conceived. God asks for no grovelling abasement. He seeks by the enfolding of His love to produce an awareness of dependence, an awareness which makes mind and heart alert, watchful for that which harms, ready for that which strengthens, outgoing and tender towards others as God has been to us. Ruskin said acutely: 'I believe that the first test of a truly great man is his humility. Really great men have a curious feeling that the greatness is not in them but through them. And they see something divine in every other man and are endlessly, incredibly merciful.'

7 Rest is peace and it dwells within. Laurence Sterne who learned the hard way, wrote over two centuries ago: 'Rest unto our souls! – 'tis all we want – the end of all our wishes and pursuits; we seek for it in titles, in riches and in pleasures – climb up after it by ambition, come down and stoop for it by avarice, try all extremes; nor is it till after many miserable experiments that we are convinced, at last, we have been seeking everywhere for it but where there is a prospect of finding it; and that is within ourselves, in a meek and lowly disposition of heart.'

8,9 The verse needs no new rendering. A felicitous translator had a part in the familiar version of the psalms. He cannot be bettered than in the simple expression linking gratitude with resolve in these verses.

10,11 The RSV does its best with these two difficult verses: 'I kept my faith even when I said, "I am greatly afflicted." I said in my consternation, "Men are all a vain hope." ' The point seems to be that, though in the extremity of distress the writer almost lost his faith, he nevertheless won through and never quite gave way. The situation, however, was complicated by the apparent helplessness of men. Or perhaps he had found friends like Job's, irritating in their judgements, sanctimonious, and without real contact with his need. Now, in new communion with God, he feels a little contrite at his harsh reaction to them. All deep sorrow is lonely. In the straits of sorrow and of spiritual conflict, the apparent helplessness of others to aid is sometimes a real agony. The old Sankey hymn touched on the point:

> *Go bury thy sorrow,*
> *The world has its share,*
> *Go bury it deeply,*
> *Go hide it with care.*

There is only One who will listen, understand and aid.

12–14 The writer turns to gratitude and its symbolic demonstration. Some act of worship seems involved. It is not known when 'the cup of blessing' (Matt. 26.27), from which the Christian communion cup descended, became part of the Paschal meal, but this verse (13) may indicate that it was known at the time this psalm was written. Both vs. 14 and 17 also indicate that some public act of worship was involved. This seems to be the best explanation.

15 'His loved ones are very precious to him and he does not lightly let them die.' Such is the Living Bible paraphrase and it catches the meaning well (see 72.14).

16–19 The joyous prayer rises to its climax. It is as though his act of public acknowledgement brings before the singer's mind the vision of the Temple, newly arising or arisen on its hill. It is a glad journey he will make to pay his vows.

Conclusion

'The highest joy to the Christian always comes through suffering. No flower can bloom in Paradise which is not transplanted from Gethsemane. No one can taste of the tree of life that has not tasted of the fruits of the tree of Calvary. The crown is after the cross' (A. Maclaren). The words quoted are perhaps not universally true. Maclaren is thinking of something more refined than happiness and it is probably true that some of the deeper satisfactions of the spirit are those which come with the morning, after some night of darkness and of pain. Such is the message of this most joyous psalm.

Read Psalm 117; Romans 15

This shortest of all the psalms, a mere two verses, is not a fragment. It does not comfortably fit on to the end of the preceding psalm, as some have suggested, nor attach relevantly to the beginning of the next. The compiler of the Psalter must have found it as a separate unit, and included it in the form in which it was used, a sort of doxology or invocation which could be used anywhere. Paul quotes the first verse together with Psa. 18.49, Deut. 32.43 and Isaiah 11.1 to show from the Old Testament that the Gentiles ('the nations') were included, along with the Jews, in the great plan of God.

118

Read Psalm 118; Nehemiah 12

Occasion and author

Some unknown poet put this hymn of praise together for a notable festive occasion – perhaps when the walls of the city were truly rising again after Nehemiah's heroic toils. Suggestions have been various – that it marked the first celebration of the Feast of Tents, when nothing but an altar had been erected (Ezra 3.1–4), the foundation laying of the second Temple (Ezra 3.8–13), the consecration of the Temple (Ezra 6.15–18) and so on. Who can know, save that it was a high occasion of praise. A careful study of the language provides support for all these suggestions.

The tone, the meaning, the spirit of the poem transcends the words. It was Luther's favourite. 'This is my own psalm,' he said, 'which I specially love . . . I have come to grips with this psalm in a special sense . . . It has done me great service on many an occasion, and has stood by me in many a difficulty, when the emperor, kings, wise men and clever were of no avail.'

The psalm shows what Luther meant.

Commentary

1–4 One can almost hear the antiphonal chanting of the massed Levitical choirs and the congregational responses in the fine strong writing of the prelude to this song. They laud the 'loving-kindness' of God. The word is one of the contributions to English made by the great Elizabethan version of the Bible. The word contains kindness, mercy, steadfastness, but should not be exchanged for any one of them.

5–9 Both Ezra's and Nehemiah's books show how true was the fact that God alone could continue the restoration. The policy of the shahs wavered, and even with the writ of the 'Great King' to support him, Nehemiah found that fellow satraps like the neighbouring Sanballat of Samaria, could take advantage of their remoteness from the centre of government to defy imperial authority.

10–14 Almost a chant, a sort of drum-roll of victory continues the story. Israel sought to establish her nationhood in her ancient land and all the frontiers of fear were alight again – Samaria, Arabia, Ammon, the Philistine remnants at Ashdod (Neh. 4.7,8).

15–18 Some unrecorded confidence sets the song afire. If they are right who set this psalm down as a hymn for the Feast of Tents, v. 15 would have special poignancy.

19–24 Verse 22 of this section has been the subject of much legend. Perhaps, in fact, it does refer to some incident in the building of the Temple when some stone, cast aside at first, on later choice proves ideal for the task of locking together a vital corner of the walls. So Israel, rejected, and now again a keystone of history. In Matt. 21.42–44 (Mark 12.10,11; Luke 20.17,18) the Lord appropriates these words and those of the verse which follows. It is significant that He thus quotes from the psalm which had formed the crowd's salutation just before (Matt. 21.9). See also Acts 4.11; I Pet. 2.7 and Eph. 2.20. Israel as 'a type' of Christ clearly impressed Peter. Isa. 28.16 forms a connecting link between the Psalm and the New Testament appropriation of its striking figure of speech. In contrast Jeremiah says of Babylon: 'They shall not take of thee a stone for a corner . . .' And how true is this. Babylon made some contribution to history, but Palestine has been a corner-stone of two millennia of history.

25–29 The RSV avoids the difficulty of 'binding the sacrifice to the horns of the altar' by rendering: 'Bind the festal procession with branches, even up to the horns of the altar.' The vital word means 'festival'. In Mal. 3.2 it means 'festal sacrifice'. The RSV makes some sense by imagining such a procession as that which greeted the Lord when he entered Jerusalem, as given a green and leafy unity, like the advancing forest in the closing scene of *Macbeth*, by the host of palm fronds carried by them. The rendering 'branches' or 'boughs' instead of cords is linguistically warranted, and the word rendered 'bind' is used in I Kings 20.14 and 2 Chron. 13.3 for the process of ordering an army for battle. The possibility of the RSV rendering is thus open. If some processional is here envisaged this is plausible. 'Join the procession with leafy boughs . . .' says the NASB. 'With branches in your hands draw up in procession . . .' runs the JB. The Messianic conclusion of the psalm is thus enhanced.

119

Read the whole Psalm

Occasion and author

In Book Five of the Psalms we can almost see the editor at work. He found himself with several smaller groups, as we have seen, to arrange. There were the Egyptian Hallel (Pss. 113–118); the Great Hallel (Pss. 120–136); perhaps a recognized grouping called the Songs of Ascent; and along with these sundry pieces (for example Psa. 143) which partake of the character of earlier collections, but which for some reason were not earlier placed. Then there was a collection of sayings about God's Word, the anthology, perhaps by many, even 176 hands, which we call Psa. 119. The editor placed this special piece right in the middle of his book. Perhaps this was done for no other reason than the mere convenience of handling. A papyrus or vellum roll was unwound from a stick in one hand on to a stick in the other. A reader called upon to read the longest of the psalms would be helped in the physical task if the weight in each hand was, as far as possible, equalized.

Like two earlier psalms in this book (111 and 112) this long psalm is alphabetical. This device is an aid to memory. Under each of the letters of the Hebrew alphabet, the same number of verses are placed. It is perhaps possible to trace a sequence and development of thought but the train is elusive and memorizing becomes a matter of extreme difficulty. Ruskin speaks somewhere of walking to Marble Arch reciting this psalm, so the feat is not impossible, and people of other and especially remote centuries, relied upon and used memory much more than is done today.

The Fifth Book, on the whole, appears more closely aligned to liturgical use. The hymnbook of the second Temple was taking shape and the Song of the Word, set in the midst of this book reflects the growing zeal for the Bible, which had been the cement of the exiled remnant, which, in default of all else, temple, ritual, sacrifice, functioning priesthood, had been put together from memory, precariously preserved fragments of manuscript, and the collective recollection of the race. The value of the Word could not be doubted. It contained the sustenance of an uprooted people, their treasury of hope, the surviving value of the past and confidence in the future.

This psalm was probably put together from his own words and those of others by a rabbi in exile, a man, it might be guessed, who survived to return with Ezra and work upon the compiling of the whole collection of the psalms. From the themes which emerge it might be assumed that the writer, editor or compiler, was also the author of Psa. 1. He was deeply preoccupied with happiness in the truest and highest sense of the word – 'blessedness' in the biblical sense. He had suffered persecution (21,23) from overbearing

90

authority (61,69). His faith had at times staggered (6,22,31) and he was under pressure to give in, adapt, like Esther and Mordecai, to an enfolding society, and forget (36,37). Such stress grieved him (25,28) for he saw that the service of the Lord and the destiny of his people demanded the committal of the whole life and the building, indeed, of an absorbing way of life on the Word of God (10,34,58,69, 145). Perhaps here is a document of the beginning of Pharisaism, in the finest sense of the word, when determined and pious Jews responded to the trials of exile by laying hold on the laws of the Lord. Therein lay an instinct for preservation which was justified and illustrated in history. The synagogue as an institution was built by men like this and convictions implicit in their collected words.

Commentary
ALEPH
1 Here is the touch of the Beautitudes and of Psa. 1. Who is the truly happy man? The answer is: they who live their life within the pattern of God's will . . . who live according to the law of the Lord.
2 After the pattern of Hebrew poetry, the same thought is repeated, but with changed emphasis. Verse 2 insists that 'walking according to the Law' is a matter which demands committal. Such conduct has roots and springs deep in a surrendered personality. If this writer wrote Psa. 1 he was a formal poet skilled in the patterning of thoughts and words. He has achieved a parallelism within each verse, and between the first two verses.
3,4 Conduct, not profession, is the test, and obedience is the colour of such a life.

The question is answered: Happiness is obedience. The theme traverses the Bible from Eden onwards . . . 'Thou shalt not . . .' 'To obey is better than sacrifice . . .' 'Not everyone . . . but he that does the will of my Father . . .' And listen to Christian thinkers from three different centuries. First, Montaigne, the French essayist, who died in 1592: 'The first law that ever God gave to man was a law of obedience. It was a commandment pure and simple wherein man had nothing to enquire after or dispute for as much as to obey is the proper office of a rational soul acknowledging a heavenly Superior Benefactor.' And Bossuet the great preacher (1627–1704): 'Thirty years of our Lord's life were hidden in these words of the Gospel – "He was subject unto them" '. And William Paley, the Churchman (1743–1805): 'One very common error misleads the opinion of mankind, that authority is pleasant and submission painful. The reverse is nearer to the truth: Command is anxiety; obedience is ease.'
5 We begin to see a progress in the section. The principle has been stated. It is a rigorous command. At the thought the writer fears that he may fail and lifts a prayer which proves that his obedience, at any rate, was rooted in the heart, a matter of most intimate resolve.
6 There is no shame for such a man. He walks, not in pride, but in calm and confidence.
7 Such a life is no sudden achievement. There is much to learn of the will of God. Each day has its lessons. Night by night speaks knowledge (19.2). The Living Bible may be right when it renders: 'After you have corrected me, I will thank you by living as I should.' Let us learn the lessons quickly and apply them.

8 'I will obey! Oh, do not forsake me and let me slip back into sin again.' This is what Paul means when he bids the Philippians translate the salvation they have accepted into the stuff of life with reverence and self-distrust.

The question is answered. Happiness can be found, but it costs all that man has, in earnest faith and diligent following.

BETH

9 The theme of this section follows the last thought. Man being what he is does not find obedience easy. It demands alertness, says this verse. The ambush lurks. The path must be scanned, its perils foreseen. There is a guide. Somewhere, for those who diligently search, the Bible contains the sure answer.

10 It demands wholeheartedness. Lukewarmness revolts the Lord (Rev. 3.15,16). The promise is only to the truly surrendered (Matt. 5.6). Only those who search with the whole drive and passion of the heart and mind will surely find (Jer. 29.13). There is no blessing on the shallow, the fickle, the half-hearted.

11 The secret is to house the Word of God in the depths of the being where all originates. An evil man speaks out of the evil which he has stored up in his personality (Luke 6.45). It is what lies at the source which ultimately builds the person.

12 God's Spirit housed in such a temple (2 Cor. 6.16) similarly permeates and transforms, but, whereas evil so domiciled rots its dwelling, God, making Himself manifest in the life and person of a man, makes that man into that which God, his Creator, ultimately intended him to be.

13 A test lies in speech. The man who is owned of God finds the reality invade his language in grace of speech, courtesy and testimony, in the wider meaning of that word.

14 That is what it means to be truly rich. The Prodigal's brother missed this point in his dour resentful service. He had no joy in his obedience.

15 A mind permeated by God's thinking is not a mind obsessed but a mind liberated, guided, steadied.

16 And can such a mind be other than a good and joyous mind?

GIMEL

17 Note the pain of mind and heart which colours some of the little prayers which form today's reading. Bewilderment and agonized questioning are part of the spiritual pilgrimage. The psalms are full of the sufferer's cry of anguish, and appeal for enlightenment, for some glimmer of meaning in life's enigma of pain. In this psalm the writer is sure that the answer lies somewhere in God's Word. This man has known deprivation and fear for his life (see also vs. 25,37,40,50,77,88).

18 He has known times of darkness when understanding of God's plan and purpose eluded him. He longs for relevance and insight –

> *There are days so dark that I cannot see*
> *Through the mist of His wise design . . .'*

19 There is loneliness when the Word of God seems contradicted by the overwhelming evidence of life, triumphant evil, and the brazen heaven of a seemingly silent God. Nothing has meaning and faith seems cheated.

20 'My soul yearns all the time for thee to intervene' (Moffatt). This is a grim section. Exile was pressing heavily on devoted hearts 'beside the waters of Babylon'.

Thus the first half of Gimel. Then, as in Aleph, the mood changes. (This section seems unusually autobiographical.)

21–24 This surely is the memory of a humiliating experience before some biased and pagan court. All authority was not exercised against the Jews as the upright Gallio saw fit to exercise it. The leaders of the uprooted minority would be those charged before the city judges should the prejudice of the mob (see Acts 19) lead to a demonstration against them, and the appeasement of popular hatred by some show of legal action. Such evil has not yet left the world. If this psalmist was also a rabbi, it could be that he had to endure the contempt (22), the calumny and the persecution of the court (23). He was, it seemed, preserved (21), steadied in his defence (23), and found God's Word an advocate and adviser. Thus to use and experience the steadying strength of God's Word, it should be remembered, one would need to weave its precepts closely with the mind. To memorize Scripture is salutary for the Christian. Observe that the victim still feels soiled by his experience. 'Take away from me disgrace and scorn' (AAT) he cries, as though some befouled garment had to be stripped from him to give a sense of cleanliness. There are experiences which can do that to a clean and upright man. If the risk can be confined to time and place, then such times, such places are to be shunned by the child of God who desires to avoid the taint and stain of evil.

DALETH

This section is carefully constructed round the recurring contrast of desire and fulfilment, the psalmist's inadequacy and God's completeness, summed up verse by verse with confession and related petition. Like its predecessors, this section has a visible unity complete in itself. The writer or compiler has been shaken by pain, trouble or depression, and seeks life in the Word.

25 'My soul is bowed to the dust,' says Moffatt. 'I lay in dust,' as George Matheson put it, 'life's glory dead'. 'Give me life', 'revive me', he begs. There is no cheap and easy way out of such a pit, shallow hymns notwithstanding. It is not a case of 'Get down on your knees, till your heart's overflowing with joy'. Prayer is a battleground where evil is met face to face. To fight is none the less a duty, and victory a promise. God understands –

> *He knows the bitter, weary way,*
> *Those that weep and those that pray,*
> *The endless striving day by day –*
> *He knows, He knows it all.*

26 He has spread his life before God, confessed his sin and sought to put all the record right. He has numbered, surveyed, examined the acts and events of life, and this is a prime exercise of prayer. His conclusion is that he needs more insight into the ways of God. 'Understanding', the finding of reason and significance in life, is a fruit of prayer and meditation. This psalm often returns to the thought (34,73,125, 144,169).

27 When a man understands, he can preach, and not effectively before.

93

28 In many psalms the undulation of battle is visible. The suppliant seems to be gaining the victory when another wave of attackers sweeps in. 'Nerve me as thou hast promised' (Moffatt), is a gasp of failing strength.

29 'Keep me from being false to thee' (Moffatt), he continues. A prerequisite of prayer and victory is utter sincerity. It is impossible to deceive God. Note that this is the second of the four times that 'way' is used in this section. There is a 'way of God's precepts' a 'way of falsehood', a 'way of truth' and a 'way of God's commandments'. In other words God's will, the practice of deceit and lying, the search for truth and devotion to it, and the diligent observance of God's commands, can form a pattern of life.

30 It is a matter of choice and steadfast desire. 'A life filled with truth is my choice.' God's view of right and wrong is what determines mine. The prayer of the last verse becomes the determination of this. Not to have compromised, not to have falsely shown Christ, to have kept the faith, should be the prayer of every Christian.

31 'I cling to your ordinances, Lord; let me not be disgraced' (Harrison).

32 To 'enlarge the heart' means to deepen understanding, to sharpen discernment, to make life more real in all that matters. Professor Herbert Butterfield's conclusion of his *Christianity and History*, now almost thirty years old, comes to mind. He writes: 'In regard to some of the most important things in life it is remarkable how little human beings know their liberty – how little they realize that the grand discoveries of the various inductive sciences still leave us free to range with the upper parts of our minds. In these days also when people are so much the prisoners of systems – especially the prisoners of those general ideas which mark the spirit of the age – it is not always realized that belief in God gives us greater elasticity of mind, rescuing us from too great subservience to intermediate principles, whether these are related to nationality or ideology or science. I have nothing to say at the finish except that if one wants a permanent rock in life and goes deep enough for it, it is difficult for historical events to shake it. There are times when we can never meet the future with sufficient elasticity of mind, especially if we are locked in the contemporary systems of thought. We can do worse than remember a principle which both gives us a firm Rock and leaves us the maximum elasticity for our minds: the principle: Hold to Christ, and for the rest be totally uncommitted.'

One of the privileges of the later years of life is to discover with delight that the mind need not age. Its pleasures and its worth can consciously enlarge and create a deeper conviction that a divine process is at work that the body's passing cannot quench.

HE

The alphabetical pattern of this section was easy to contrive. There is a form of the Hebrew verb called Hiphil. By means of the prefixing of the letter 'he' which heads these eight verses, a verb was given a causative turn. Thus 'learn' in Hiphil can be turned into 'teach' by a simple prefix. 'Show' can be the Hiphil of 'see' (e.g. 'caused thee to see', Deut 34.4, KJV). Each verse of this section could thus be made in English, to begin with the word 'cause'. Ronald Knox who, with some damage to style and occasionally to meaning, undertakes the difficult task of making his sections follow an English alphabetical pattern, must have regretted that he could not make this his C section. He is down to E at this point.

33 '. . . and I will follow step by step,' Moffatt translates. There is no other way to learn the things of God – or the things of man. 'One step enough for me,' says Newman's hymn, and so it must be.

34 Almost responsively this verse carries on the theme. The 'whole heart' must be given to any kind of quest. Only the determined and the tenacious achieve any sort of goal.

35 Say the same truth in another way and such a verse as this emerges. To 'delight' in learning is inevitably to learn. 'Make me to go . . .' (KJV) implies discipline, and without discipline neither learning nor teaching is possible. It is not without significance that 'discipline' is the Latin for 'learning'.

36 'Incline my heart . . .' (KJV), 'Turn my mind . . .' (Harrison), 'Help me to prefer . . .' (LB), all imply God's active discipline. Discipline, on the other hand, is an affair of two. The one who accepts it must do so by an act of the surrendered will. 'Covetousness', 'gain' or 'money making', as others render it, was no doubt visible in Babylon. Some of the exiles had carved out a place in pagan society. There were greedy and subservient Jews like Mordecai, ready to sacrifice his relative to the harem of a foul king. The Septuagint renders the word by the Greek *pleonexia* which means 'striving for more'. Barclay has collected the New Testament occurrences of the word. He says: 'The word occurs in Mark 7.22; Luke 12.15; Rom. 1.29; 2 Cor. 9.5; Eph. 4.19; 5.3; Col. 3.5; 1 Thess. 2.5; 2 Pet. 2.3,14. The regular KJV translation is "covetousness". Once, in Eph. 4.19 the KJV translates it "greediness". The RSV retains "covetousness" in most passages but translates "greedy practice" in Eph. 4.19 and "greed" in the 2 Pet. passages. Moffatt varies more. He retains "covetousness" in Luke 12.15, but his regular translation is "lust", which he uses in seven of the passages. Once in 1 Thess. 2.5, he uses "self-seeking".' It is an ugly word full of grasping, greed, avarice. Avarice was the vice which the backslidden, who had 'forgotten Jerusalem', entertained. It is the corroding force of today. In a talk given by the poet T. S. Eliot from the BBC in February, 1937: 'Perhaps the dominant vice of our time,' said Eliot, 'will prove to be avarice. There is something wrong with our attitude to money. The acquisitive rather than the creative instincts are encouraged.'

A little reflection could satisfy us that the prophecy is coming true. Enough, it has been said, 'is always a little more than a man has.' Hence dissatisfaction and corroding jealousies. An urge for more, regardless of justice or justification, by tactics militant or subtle, can destroy peace, promote a ceaseless raiding of the nation's wealth, and bring about a many-sided competition which spawns ever more restlessness and takes all tranquillity from life.

37 'Make my eyes overlook, or pass to one side . . .' is the literal meaning and we sometimes long for a strong, great loving hand to take our fascinated gaze from the unreal things, the futilities and tinsel of this world. Such gaze is death. Of this bemusement the 'lost tribes', those who never came back from exile, died. Hence the ending: 'Give me life in thy ways.'

38 Perhaps the sight of the worldly-minded stirs a fear. What, after all, if the Mordecais are right, and there is folly in believing the promises of God?

He cries: 'Make your promise come true – the promise given to those who reverence your name.'

39 The reproach he feared was that he had followed an empty dream. It hovered, it still hovers, on the edge of the mind when a man sacrifices much for God and allows what the world thinks splendid to slip from his fingers. The speakers in Malachi put it well (3.14–18). One writer in the Talmud said that it was 'the chaff of Israel' who returned – the reverse of the truth. If the guess is right that the compiler of this psalm also rounded off the Psalter with Psa. 1, then the theme of that psalm and some of its imagery, could be explained.

40 As often the last verse sums up.

WAW

Besides being a letter of the alphabet, *waw* is also the Hebrew for 'and', attached to the beginning of the next word. It was easy, then, for the compiler to effect his alphabetic pattern in this verse.

41 Paul may have had this verse in mind when he wrote Rom. 12.1. The mercies of God are manifold and every person of faith can list them. Moffatt renders: 'Let thy love come to my rescue . . .' All salvation is 'according to His Word'. There is no other authority.

42 Again there intrudes the consciousness of the watching pagan world. Remember Ezra's revealing word (8.22). It must have been a sensitive point among people inclined to measure God's favour by success and material advantage (a matter which the Exile went far to purge from their thinking), to see themselves a despised minority, with Marduk triumphant in his high temple, and the Jews despised, neglected, as the common sneer would be, by their helpless God. The psalmist longs for a convincing answer. 'Then can I face my revilers' (Moffatt).

43 In a word 'keep me preaching, with something to preach about' (51.13).

44 And so, he continues, almost revealing a suppressed fear, my own faith will stand secure.

45 Therein lies liberty, for the truth makes free.

46,47 Was the writer an officer of Ezra charged with the frightening task of appearing before the king? The Persian successors to the Babylonian dynasty were at first more humane than the tyrants they had destroyed, but Ahasuerus in Esther's story, is illustration enough of the terrors with which they surrounded the throne.

48 The meaning of the Hebrew word *caph* was noted on the last verse of Psa. 78. *Caph* was the cupped, receiving hand, the gesture being that common with some Bantus. The two hands receive a gift, courteously cupped.

The section closes with the psalmist 'meditating' on God's commands. Had Adam done this, would he have fallen? It is thus that obedience becomes intelligent. Simonides' epitaph on the fallen of Thermopylae's brave stand illustrates the point:

> *Tell Sparta, stranger passing by,*
> *That here obedient to her words we lie.*

The Greek runs literally 'persuaded by her sayings'. The Greek liked to understand why he obeyed. So do all intelligent people. Hence the need to think.

ZAYIN

The last section raised the question of Israel's hope – the old promises of restoration. It was getting late and the weaker exiles were finding their faith flagging. Hence the link between the first verse and the preceding section. The tone is taken on from the first verse. The section also seems intensely biographical.

49   There is no salvation in despair. Hope is life. Where there is no hope there is no endeavour. Whatever enlarges hope exalts courage. The Bible is a book of hope because it refuses to accept death and annihilation. Life to be liveable must have a purpose and a goal. Hope infuses both. And this small life is not large enough to contain all that we hope (John 6.68). Said Khayyam:

> *The Worldly Hope men set their Hearts upon*
> *Turns ashes – or it prospers; and anon,*
> *Like Snow upon the Desert's dusty Face*
> *Lighting a little hour or two – is gone.*

That is why, as Paul saw, we must have unearthly hope (1 Cor. 15.12–19). 'Mighty hopes,' said Tennyson, 'make us men.'

50   Only in the Word is such hope. It 'puts life into him', zest and meaning infuse the misery of the long day. 'Comfort' was needed. The word occurs twice in this section. We need it. That is why Isa. 40 is one of the most heart-warming utterances in the Bible.

51   Again comes the trial which humanity finds it most difficult to bear. Ridicule is the first and last argument of fools. The shattered Jewish nation had to bear its burden beyond deserving. 'What do these feeble Jews?' sneered Sanballat, satrap of Samaria, when Nehemiah set to work on the walls of Jerusalem. The response was like that of this psalm – to set it before God and carry on (Neh. 4.1–6).

52   The psalmist found comfort in memory and fixing faith on past promise and deliverance.

53   He shrank, too, from the spectacle of blasphemy and vice spread about him. A man should beware when evil ceases to horrify him. Pamela Hansford Johnson, writing on the Moors Murder Trial in Britain (she calls her book *On Iniquity*) makes this point strongly. She quotes a young Englishman who was in Nuremberg when the Nazi campaign against the Jews was raging. The exiles, in Germany as in Babylon, were suffering humiliation and cruelty in the streets. 'The first time,' he said, 'it was such a shock, I felt so sick, that I simply took to my heels down the next side turning. The second occasion I felt it was my duty to see what was going on, so I stopped just for a minute. I felt as sick as ever, and did so the third time I tried to watch. On the fourth I stood in that jeering crowd for quite a while. It seemed awful, but not quite as awful as before, almost as if it was a play. I told myself that this was only because I was getting more objective, was able to make a true observation of what was being done, so I could warn people when I got home. Suddenly I realized that I was in serious danger of becoming acclimatized to feel all this was part of my life, the way things happened. And then I took to my heels for a second time, and I went back to England as soon as I could get my bags packed.'

Pope expresses the same thought in his *Essay on Man*:

> *Vice is a monster of so frightful mien,*
> *As, to be hated needs but to be seen;*
> *Yet seen too oft, familiar with her face,*
> *We first endure, then pity, then embrace.*

54 The writer has been abroad in the pagan streets. He goes home and opens the roll of the book. It is growing as this exile and that remember more, or secure some manuscript. The 'house of my pilgrimage', of course, could simply mean 'the land of my exile', but a home of sorts can sum it up, a humble place in a ghetto street. But he still has a song to sing. That is the point G. K. Chesterton makes magnificently in the poem already quoted – *The Ballad of the White Horse*. Alfred, disguised as a Wessex minstrel, sings in the pagan camp:

> *That on you is fallen the shadow,*
> *And not upon the Name;*
> *That though we scatter and though we fly,*
> *And you hang over us like the sky,*
> *You are more tired of victory,*
> *Than we are tired of shame.*

> *That though all lances split on you,*
> *All swords be heaved in vain,*
> *We have more lust again to lose*
> *Than you to win again.*

And see Acts 16.25.

55 Night is more than the mere hours of darkness. There is the 'dark night of the soul' – those hours of wakeful blackness, when the sombre burdens of life press heavily on the spirit. There is One only at such a moment to trust. He is always within reach.

56 'This is my blessed lot – because I have obeyed.'

CHETH

57 'Obeyed'? This is the link between the sections.

58 Grace and mercy are his craving.

59 In the light of a prayer so audacious, he examines his life. This is how to live for God – in rigid self-examination (John 3.21), bringing all life into the light in which all deeds are truly seen, and being ready to walk where God wills.

60 When conviction of right or wrong takes form and shape in such honest self-examination, there is one course only open – with no delay to hurry to put good into action and set right that which is wrong. This is what it means, in the arming of the Christian soldier, to clasp tight the 'belt of truth' (Eph. 6.14).

61 Such a stand is a declaration of war, promptly taken up. The 'noose of the wicked' is prompt to entangle, but a man can still stand firm armed by the knowledge that he is right with God.

62 And he can thus triumph in the midst of the darkness. The verse echoes v. 55. Zayin and Cheth are, in fact, closely related.

63 A vast reward, of which most Christians are conscious, is the fellowship of kindred minds, bridging cultures, passing through and over all barriers of class and race, as no other interest, ideology or allegiance can.

64 The Lord is not confined, in conclusion, by any form of frontier. God dwelt in Babylon as He dwelt in Jerusalem. He knew no limitations.

TETH

The section is quieter in its tone, the old theme noted in other psalms – emotion recollected in tranquillity.

65 In a verse –

His love in time past
Forbids me to think
He'll leave me at last
In trouble to sink.

66 'Teach me good sense and knowledge for I rely on your commandments' (JB). That is, teach me intelligently to apply what I have believed. A man has brains to use, reason is a guide. Out of the preoccupation with the Word of this time in history, arose Pharisee and scribe with a task to do, the task of propagating and making known God's law. Had those who so nobly began, and who so valiantly performed this task, but followed the precept of this verse, the absurdities and perils of later Pharisaism would have been avoided. The lesson is still to be learned. The precept never ceases to be relevant.

67 Affliction is a 'rough schoolmaster', to adapt a phrase of Thucydides. The writer is beginning, through the murk, to catch the vision of God's truth. Why had he permitted the sorrow of the Exile to fall? It was a discipline allowed and the purpose is emerging in the writer's mind.

68 God never permits anything unless it can be transformed into good. The simple premise is that God is good. Therefore He cannot do evil. If He fails or wills not to act when evil seems triumphant, it is only because He sees good emerging ultimately from the situation. It cannot be otherwise, and the task of the afflicted is to co-operate, to search for the good, and to promote its emergence.

69 'Proud men bespatter me with lies' (Moffatt). Their words and falsehoods are like the stains of the street on the garments. 'Insolent men have plastered falsehoods on me.' The insolent are typical pagans, swollen (as the root of the word implies) with self-esteem.

70 'Their minds are gross and dull, but I thrill to thy law' (Moffatt). A fat heart, arteries clogged and narrowed, is a malfunctioning heart, and soon will be a dead heart. It is curious to see the Hebrew metaphor(KJV)touching a truth of pathology.

71 The verse picks up like a refrain the significance of trouble (67). 'It was good for me to have to suffer, the better to learn your statutes.'

72 Summing up: there is real wealth in what God says, a treasure beyond the computations of material riches. 'To do the will of Jesus – that is rest', as Bickersteth's hymn put it.

YOD

Affliction and persecution fruitfully endured continues to be the theme. There is an autobiography again in this section.

73 God created wonderfully the body. What of the wonder of the mind? The mind which contemplates and thrills to the marvels and beauties of nature is greater than the inanimate universe which stirs its awe:

> *Ah God! to see the branches stir*
> *Across the moon at Grantchester!*

The reverence overwhelming a poet's living, responding mind, is more a theme for marvel than the moon's disc swinging high . . . Therefore, says the psalmist, let the One who has created the instrument of thought, also fire and fill the understanding.

74 Gifts are for sharing. Said the hymn of Charles Wesley:

> *O let me commend my Saviour to you,*
> *I set to my seal that Jesus is true . . .*

The 'glory of the lighted mind', of Saul Kane's phrase in *The Everlasting Mercy*, is communicable.

75 He has proved something, seen a new purpose, a strengthening significance, and must pass the knowledge on. It is the preoccupation of every true scholar to propagate and communicate his discoveries.

76,77 The Lord permitted us to pray that we be led not into testing. The psalmist has learned much from his late affliction, but he is not to be expected to enjoy the pain. Hence this tender prayer: 'Now please let your love comfort me, as you have promised your servant' (JB). 'Let thy compassions reach me that I may live' (Harrison).

78 The proud, or the insolent, again invade his mind. The arrogant denizens of the great empire, like the Romans of New Testament days, must have been a burden to the Jews, themselves conscious of the uniqueness of their race, and even tempted, in their lesser moments, to be proud of it.

79,80 Perhaps there is a recognition in these two verses of some new call to leadership or responsibility. It is no unworthy ambition to seek to rally the good, as long as the task is accepted in humility. And this is so. The suppliant begs for a sound (blameless, undivided, perfect) heart and a clear conscience in a task well done.

CAPH

This Hebrew letter is named after the cupped hand – and over the whole section hovers the Hand that grips.

81 The years slip by. Life seems worthless, while all that the nation stood for lay crumbling under the weeds. There is a note of desperation in the closing words. 'Hope deferred makes the heart sick' – and hope deferred is hope that recedes. The mood is desperate.

82 The vision, once so bright, is fading. He calls for comfort. That word is always rendered in the Latin Vulgate by *confortare*, which by its prefix and derivation suggest 'strength from a presence'. 'I can do all things in Christ who strengthens me' – 'in eo qui me confortat' – in Him who is with me to make strong (Phil. 4.13).

83 A vivid image of a leather goatskin of wine left to mature in an upper chamber where the hearthsmoke passed, aged with apparent neglect.

84 The days pass and God appears inordinately to tarry. The verse is paralleled in many Davidic psalms. Such discipline Abraham, Moses, David and Paul knew. It seems to be an essential discipline for the chosen of God, for men set aside for a task. 'How long, O Lord, how long?'

85 Meanwhile the wicked rejoice in the apparent abandonment of the good. Their sneers are backed by treachery.

86 There are moments when the arrogance and evil and the longing for vindication become unbearable. Doubt strikes, and the most awful doubt of all is the fear that the vision which so brightly lured and held the mind is after all a dream.

87 The evil man had almost won. God's Word alone preserved. This is historic fact. The Scriptures saved the nation through these trying and damaging days.

88 Evil destroys. God gives life. Let Him so give. A sad section. Faith holds but he has been near defeat.

LAMED

A quieter section with a quiet note of confidence follows.

89 We are back with Psa. 8. The heavens declare the glory of God. Immutable laws swing the planets and the stars. Pluto was discovered because of minute variations in another planet's course. Taking for certain that variation must have a reason, an astronomer, by pure calculation, discovered where to look, and the explanation was waiting to be found. All that appears awry in life has similar explanation. The moral law which is interwoven with the texture of history and of life, is as precise and perfect as the physical laws in the natural creation.

90 So it has always been. God does not grow up, as Aeschylus imagined, groping in his Prometheus plays for what eluded his questing mind. He has always been the same in the past.

91 And as He was in the past so He is in the present and with no exceptions. It is clear that the writer's mind is probing for a reason. God seemed to bring His people through disaster in the past. Why not today?

92 The faith that God must be the same, must ultimately act and vindicate the good has been the only sustenance through catastrophe and temptation to despair. 'I would have died in my misery' (Moffatt).

93 That realization is firm and shall continue firm. He owes his life to God's sustaining Word or else despair had killed him – a tremendous statement of faith.

94 This crystallizes into a petition: 'I belong to You. Rescue me, for I have looked carefully for Your commands' (Harrison). Alert, ready, he waits. God alone seems to tarry, but there is no sound of petulant reproach.

95 The foes await like ambushed evil along the track. He will walk in confidence.

96 All that man can do has its limits – God has none. 'Look where I may, all good things must end; only thy law is wide beyond measure' (Knox).

This man was like Paul (2 Tim. 1.12).

MEM

The mood is changing to one of praise and wonder at the wisdom the Word gives.

97 This verse sets the tone for the section.

98 Wisdom is the distillation of knowledge, that understanding which comes from the mind's sifting of accumulated fact. Wisdom is at once the simplification and the consummation of knowledge.

Such is the role of the Bible. England once knew it.

The testimony of two historians comes to mind . . . It was a century ago last year that John Richard Green published his famous *Short History of the English People*. His Eighth Chapter on Puritan England opened with a notable sentence: 'No greater moral change ever passed over a nation than passed over England during the years which parted the middle of the reign of Elizabeth from the meeting of the Long Parliament. England became the people of a book, and that book was the Bible.' Green describes the public reading of Bishop Bonner's Bibles placed for that purpose in St. Paul's. In church and home minds were leavened with a new literature. He continues: 'Annal, war-song and psalm, biography, the mighty voices of prophets, the parables of evangelists, stories of mission journeys, of perils by sea and among the heathen, philosophic arguments, apocalyptic visions, were all flung broadcast over minds unoccupied for the most part by any rival learning.' Green shows eloquently the profound effect this all had on language, thought and literature. 'But,' he goes on, 'far greater was its effect upon the character of the people at large. Elizabeth might silence or tune the pulpits. It was impossible for her to silence or tune the great preachers of justice, and mercy and truth who spoke from the book which she had again opened for her people . . . The whole temper of the nation felt the change. A new moral and religious impulse spread through all the land . . . The whole nation became in fact a Church. The great problems of life and death, whose questionings found no answer in the higher minds of Shakespeare's day, pressed for an answer not only from noble and scholar, but from farmer and shopkeeper in the age which followed him . . .' They found their answers in the Bible.

And a brief paragraph from George Macaulay Trevelyan's *English Social History*, which appeared in 1938. Trevelyan, Lord Macaulay's great-nephew, spoke of the beneficent work of the British and Foreign Bible Society in its early years, and concludes: 'Though much was lacking in the organized education of that age, very many people of all classes at the time of Waterloo knew the Bible with a familiarity which raised their imaginations above the level of that insipid vulgarity which the modern multiplicity of printed matter tends rather to increase than to diminish.'

99,100 The Word makes him wiser, he claims, than his enemies, fed on the myths of paganism, than his teachers, and people of past generations. The two latter claims are not extravagantly made. This man may have lived through the major part of the exile, and seen the emergence of understanding in the school of suffering that gave final meaning to ancient prophecy. It is often the case that prophecy is only seen clearly when the fulfilment is before the eyes. Observe John the Baptist and the disciples (Luke 24.25–27; John 1.30–34; 16.12,13).

101–104 Obedience is the best tutor. The Word withholds its meaning unless it is obeyed. To begin with reservations is not to find significance. To begin with desire to learn and an open heart is to discover truth (John 7.17). Then the Bible acts, gives that alertness, insight and apprehension of the truth which steers the feet from error.

NUN
105 The link with Mem is clear. The closing verse of one section inspires the opening verse of the next. 'God's Word,' wrote Dr. J. R. Miller, 'a guiding light is a lamp to our feet, not a sun flooding a hemisphere. It is not meant to shine upon miles of road, but in the darkest night it will show us the next step, and then another, and thus onward till it brings us out into the clear shining of the coming day.'

106,107 The autobiographical mood invades the theme again and turns us back to the unanswerable question of how this psalm was composed. Did 176 different people each contribute a verse, youth and age together, each writing from the experience of the day? Or was there a smaller group, according to the letters of the Hebrew alphabet? Or did one writer spend many years, setting aside, as the Spirit prompted, some tiny petition rising from the day's experience? Somehow a range of passionate human emotion, aspiration, joy, and sorrow wove itself into a psalm about the Word. Is not the whole Bible a similar record? God's dealings with man, at any rate, form its theme.

108 This is rather a beautiful and unusual definition of prayer. Prayer is not an attempt to wrench things out of the hand of a God who is far more willing to give than we are to receive. Stories like that of 'Praying Hyde', who accompanied C. S. Finney in his preaching tours, distort the meaning of prayer. The note of agony and pain, of urgency and something near despair does indeed invade prayer, and the Psalter illustrates that fact as nothing else. But it is good to remember that God regards our ill-formed and ill-informed utterance as a species of sacrifice.

109 Render: 'I carry my life in my hand continually'. This was a hard fact of life for the poor and the alien. Note the interpretation of Psa. 137 given below.

110–112 Again the thought arises that the writer was a Jewish leader, always responsible in a pagan society for the behaviour of his people, continually exposed to peril. See Acts 17.5–9.

SAMECH
113 This verse in the KJV badly misses the meaning. He says: 'Half-hearted ones I hate'. 'I detest people of uncertain allegiance,' says Harrison. These are the people of divided heart of Jas. 1.8. And the same rare word occurs in Elijah's ringing word on Carmel (1 Kings 18.21). 'How long are you to limp along on two opinions' – as if one leg was shorter than another. These are the people Dante describes in Canto 3 of the *Inferno*, a misty crowd blown along behind a drifting banner. 'I would not have believed that death could have undone so many,' he says. His guide explains that they were those who had never come down firmly either for good or evil, the men of no allegiance. In Babylon there were no doubt many who waited to see where advantage lay, especially after the Persian conquest. Would it be best to go to Jerusalem and hardship when the time was ripe, or to stay in the

comfort of a land they had come to know, to follow a dream or clasp reality? Such people, and this is Dante's point, have never known really what it is to be alive.

114 The familiar image of the rocky fortress and the shield, so common in David's psalms, emerges again.

115 The waverers of the earlier strong word are back in view again. Allegiance to truth can divide and separate.

116 To take sides always stirs a doubt. 'Am I right? Shall I be shown to be right?' But all good is made of valiant choices.

117 To stand alone for good is never to stand absolutely alone. There is One to uphold.

118 All who 'swerve from Thy will' (Moffatt), who 'deviate from Thy commandments' (Harrison) can expect rejection. Our committal must be absolute. 'Their notions end in nothing,' says Moffatt drily, concluding the verse. And how true. To make some attempt to 'conserve the essential meaning' of Scripture, while rejecting its truth and authority, is inevitably to end with nothing. Authority is the right to be believed. That which is untrue cannot command obedience. The Bible has relevance and authority only if it is true, if it finds us, as Coleridge once put it, 'at greater depths of our being than any other book.' To swerve from this is to lose all the Bible can do.

119 Dross is the scum thrown off in the smelting of ore. The exiled Jews were enduring such a fire (Ezek. 22.18–22).

120 Such words as he has felt compelled to write overawe the psalmist. The sudden fear sweeps over him that, as others have failed, so may he.

AYIN

121–128 The mood of anxiety deepens and this section reads very like one of the more sombre of the Davidic psalms. Much of it is repetitive so the section will be treated as a whole. 'Thy servant' appears three times (122, 124,125), reminiscent of the 'Servant Songs' of Isaiah.

Opposition is strong against good men, and the oppressors (121) and the proud (122, KJV) seem to be gaining the upper hand. They often do, and nowhere as firmly as at Calvary. God seems inactive (123,126). He appears to do nothing while everything God commands is flouted (126). 'Give Your servant some comforting assurance' (122, Harrison) he pleads, and it is often a path for faith out of some dark and evil situation to watch consciously for tokens of God's love along the path, Elijah's cruse of water, and plate of cakes under the juniper tree, someone saying 'Brother Saul' . . . To feel like one peering down the road from which help should come (123), when that help is promised, but never seems to come, is weariness for the watching eyes. In the last verse *eol* the Hebrew for 'all' appears three times as though the watcher has searched his soul, and can see no explicable reason within himself why God should not appear to aid.

PE

The section is similar to the last but in a less desperate mood.

129 'Your instruction is wonderful. Therefore I gladly keep it.' The theme again is intelligent obedience.

130 'As your word unfolds it gives light and the simple understand' (JB).

There is no question among all those that afflict man that does not find an answer in the Bible somewhere. Search must be diligent, open-minded and with readiness to obey, but the answer is there. My friend, Edith Lovejoy Pierce, writes well:

> The questions were thousands of word-spears
> That pitted the mind with their pocks,
> The answer is ointment hidden
> In an alabaster box.
>
> The questions were searching and painful,
> Ruthless and bitter and hard,
> The answer is very costly,
> And it has the scent of nard.

131 A recollection of the 'hart panting for the waterbrooks'.
132 Just as wistful as the preceding verse. 'Look upon me as you once looked on men.'
133 'Make my step firm according to thy promise and let no wrong have the mastery over me' (NEB). A fine, strong prayer which might well be committed to memory.
134 It should not be forgotten in lands of liberty that 'the oppression of man' is still the daily burden of multitudes of Christians. They should not be denied our daily prayers.
135 'Restore to thy servant the smile of thy loving favour and teach him to know thy will' (Knox).
136 The verse prompts the question whether we are concerned enough over the vast evil which holds men in thrall (Lam. 3.48).

TSADE
137,138 Presuppose a righteous God, and what He decrees will necessarily be righteous.
139 The response of the faithful to a faithless world is a more zealous faithfulness.
140 The image appears to be that of v. 119 – a metal refined in the fire, the dross removed and the pure gold left.
141 Few will know the little poem written by the most classical of New Zealand poets with this verse in mind. R.A.K. Mason, both schoolboy friend and student of mine, never became a Christian, but he came near with this small poem which I know he would allow me to quote were he still here:

> Christ Jesus came to my door
> riding on an ass
> and though I am both weak and poor
> I could not let him pass.
>
> I called to him and bade him stay
> and bade him pass my porch
> and though it was all brightest day
> I lit my every torch.

Then though I am but weak and poor
and though I am but small
spilt all my wine upon my floor
wasted my unguents all.

142 The contrast is everlasting righteousness, and truth without admixture.

143,144 The crash of catastrophe again only to be understood if God can give meaning to it all.

KOPH

The whole section seems to take tone from some sudden inruption of evil glimpsed at in v. 143. Urgency is the keynote.

145 Prayer for help absorbs the whole being.

146 'I implore you to save me.'

To both prayers promise of faithfulness is pathetically attached.

147 'I rise before dawn and cry for help . . .' (RSV).

148 'I lie awake throughout the night . . .' (JB).

149 The plea is based on the known character of God. There is no need to change the lovely word which the KJV introduced into English. True, 'lovingkindness' is 'steadfast love', but is there need to change the term?

150 The pursuit is close. 'My cruel persecutors are closing in' (JB). This sense of claustrophobia is one of life's most bitter experiences.

151 But in such a moment he is conscious of Another by his side – 'one like to the Son of God' (Dan. 3.25).

152 The usual quiet ending – a device of the Greek orators.

RESH

The tone is quieter as though the last section had achieved some relief.

153,154 The theme and imagery of v. 24 is taken up. God is to be the advocate, accept a brief, as it were, from a righteous man and vindicate the victim.

155 The wicked have no such resource and deserve none.

156,157 'Many are thy mercies' is a possible rendering and that suggests that those who persecute are as many. (The same word is used in both contexts). And yet 'I have not swerved from thy testimonies' (ASV). The metaphor is again deviation from a firm straight line.

158 'Grieved' (KJV) is not a strong enough word. 'I look at the faithless with disgust' (RSV) is closer to the strength of the verb used.

159 The seeming self-righteousness of such statements has been discussed before in these studies. In an Old Testament context, and before the Person of Christ confronted and daunted the world, such a claim was possible.

160 Again the section closes with a general statement: 'Your sayings are supremely true', or as Luther puts it: 'Dein Wort ist nichts denn Wahrheit' – 'Your Word is nothing but the truth'.

SHIN

161 Persecution is back on the page again, but the psalmist stands more in awe of God's Word than he does of those who put pressure upon him to deny it. This was the position of the persecuted of the early Church.

162 The thought of the preciousness of the Word. To know its promises is to be 'like someone finding vast treasure' (JB).

163 To love truth is necessarily to hate falsehood.

164 'Seven' may signify a large number (12.6) or it may be literal. Daniel's prayer habits suggest that the exiled Jews sought discipline of life and religion as a therapy for despair (Daniel 6.10).

165 See 1 John 2.10. The point is that when the conscience is clear and the heart at peace, a man sees what he must do and does it. He has no quibbles. As the verse ends: 'There is no stumbling block for them' – nothing shall trip them in the path of duty. They know the price and pay it.

166–168 Compare Gen. 49.18. This is not a vain boast. The psalmist claims that he has wholeheartedly followed the light, and says this three times over.

TAU

169–176 The psalm ends with a cluster of verses which sum up its chief points. There is the repeated cry for insight, deeper understanding (169, 171), for a clear hearing (169, 170), for intervention (173,174) – in short for life. Perhaps more clearly than heretofore is the promise to spread the tidings (171,172). The last verse only, with its echo of Isa. 53.6, introduces a new image.

Conclusion

The obligation stands. The Church has the Word today, beyond the dreams of the psalmist. Such enjoyment cannot be sequestered. It must be shared. These are the days of Chesterton's prophecy . . . 'a broken heart in the breast of the world and the end of the world's desire'. The Church has the remedy, but the Church is sick for want of the Bread of God, for the Bible taught in the pulpit in place of ecstasy and anecdote, topicality and noise. The Bible, preached with authority, can still search and convict. The learned Jew with the poetry of his language alive within him who wrote a letter for Hebrew Christians put it well. 'The Word that God speaks,' he wrote, 'is alive and active; it cuts more keenly than any two-edged sword; it strikes through to the place where soul and spirit meet, to the innermost intimacies of man's being; it exposes the very thoughts and motives of a man's heart.' That is what will bring the Church to life – and a vast revival of the Faith is the one force which can save the world from the death which looms ahead. Paul said as much to young Timothy in Ephesus, the pagan city, sex-obsessed, corrupt: 'All Scripture is inspired of God, there to teach what the faith means, to correct error, to reset the direction of life, the complete equipment of the man of God . . . I adjure you, preach the Word, when you are given the opportunity or when you have to make it.'

Preached with confidence Scripture will demonstrate its own authority. It cannot be contained. It can flow into a faithful man's voice, and lay hold of his life. Studied and absorbed and passed through the screen of a man's living experience, it can stir, confront, challenge modern man, meet the problems, perplexities, the crawling ruin of this day. The Bible has the answer. Present it with sanctity, sanity, and confidence. There is no other book.

J. G. Lockhart tells of Sir Walter Scott's last days. The great writer was incapacitated by a stroke. Lockhart writes: 'He desired to be drawn into the library, and placed by the central window that he might look down upon the Tweed. Here he expressed a wish that I should read to him, and, when I asked from what book, he said – "Need you ask? There is but one." ' True. There is still but one.

120

Read Psalm 120; Ezra 1

Occasion and author

A collection of fifteen psalms in this book is called 'songs of ascent'. Later Jewish expositors derived the name from the fifteen steps from the Court of the Women to the Court of the Men and supposed that the psalms were sung on each of the steps. This looks like an aetiological myth. The Septuagint translated the title 'song of the steps' and Jerome took it into the Vulgate as 'canticum gradium' an exact translation, badly rendered into the 'song of degrees' of the KJV. There are other explanations. Some German commentators suppose that the title denoted the rhythmical character of these psalms according to which, by a certain gradation of words or ideas, an expression in one verse is taken up by the next. This is a phenomenon we have noted in other psalms, but the explanation is very difficult to support from the text. Others, following the literal translation of the title 'songs of the goings-up', say that these songs were 'pilgrim songs'. The 'going up' was from Babylon. This does not preclude the notion of 'going up' to Jerusalem on its high ridge, or to its Temple. That caravans of pilgrims to the festivals 'went up' singing is clear from Isa. 30.29. However, the notion of returning from exile or going home to Israel has laid hold of the Jewish mind. Commenting on President Sadat's demand for a half-century check on Israeli immigration, an Israeli Bulletin comments:

'Samuel Joseph Agnon, one of the greatest of modern Hebrew writers, expressed an inner reality when he said, in his address on receiving the Nobel Prize:

> "As a result of the historic catastrophe in which Titus of Rome destroyed Jerusalem and Israel was exiled from its land, I was born in one of the cities of the Exile. But I always regarded myself as one who was born in Jerusalem."

The Hebrew word for this kind of "immigration" – *Aliyah* ("ascent") – is based on the statement about the first return from Babylon over 2,500 years ago:

"Now these are the children of the province that went up out of the captivity that were in exile . . ." (Ezra 2.1).

"Went up" seems to have been meant literally, for Judea is higher than Babylonia, but the term Aliyah has taken on a deeper meaning: ascent to freedom and independence from a position of inferiority in exile. The Jew who comes to live in Israel is an *oleh*.

"Every Jew is entitled to come to this country as an oleh."

This right is recognized by the law, but it is not granted by the law, because it is an intrinsic right. Every Jew who comes as an *oleh* to live in Israel by virtue of the right of return, therefore, becomes a citizen, with all the rights and duties of a citizen, as soon as he sets foot on its soil, unless he opts out.

Aliyah is not only a modern phenomenon; it has been a constant factor in Jewish life since the beginnings of the Diaspora. Whenever the Jewish presence in the Holy Land was diminished by foreign conquest and persecution (it was never wholly extinguished), it was reinforced by repeated waves of Aliyah . . .'

The collection, whatever its origin, was made after the Restoration, as some references to the Captivity indicate. With one exception, Psa. 132, these hymns are short, and touch one line of thought. They are a trifle plaintive and muted in confidence and faith, perhaps a true expression of a people overwhelmed with toil and tension and fighting up a steep ascent to nationhood. The first psalm of the collection is also somewhat apart from the rest. It is difficult to interpret, elusive in its imagery, and can best be assigned to the years of Nehemiah when slander added gravely to the troubles of the embattled Jews. The author is, of course, unknown.

Commentary

1-4 The words are reminiscent of some Davidic psalms against the slanderers. Remembrance of times past, the familiar refuge, is again the only available ground of confidence. The sharp arrows are the punishment, envisaged perhaps as some military chastisement of Sanballat and the Arabian foes of Israel under Nehemiah's desperate leadership. The broom (KJV, 'juniper') was supposed to produce hot, long-burning coals. Jerome tells a tale of travellers making a cooking fire of the *genista monosperma*, and returning a year later found the embers still alive. The vigour of the imagery does not depend upon the truth of the story.

5-7 Meshech, probably the Moschi of Herodotus, lived far away, on the Caucasus shore of the Black Sea. The 'tents of Kedar' represent a desert tribe south of Damascus. They are symbols of remote barbarism and the writer seems to suggest that such were the savages who surrounded Israel. It is his lot to be thus hemmed in by wickedness and slander. He has travelled far for peace, and found but war. Perhaps this was the mood of some of those who battled to build the land again. Indeed the mood may be read in the stories of Ezra and Nehemiah.

Conclusion

We cannot but find in ourselves an echo sometimes of this mood. The world and its wickedness can be too much with us and we sense a longing of the heart for what Virgil calls 'the other shore'. As the old hymn had it: 'that will be glory for me.'

121

Read Psalm 121; Psalm 4

Occasion and author

The author of many of these psalms is unknown. The occasion may be imagined. Jerusalem on its hillcrest is visible against the sky as the pilgrim approaches from almost any direction. The caravan is perhaps a day's journey away, and as the song of evening worship is raised among the camp-fires, the lifted glance can pick the journey's end, crenellated against the sky, the sacred goal of their desiring.

Commentary

1,2 It is the great Creator who guides and shadows the caravan. The word 'keep' is the keyword of this whole psalm, six times repeated in the last five verses, a fine drumming repetition, lost in the KJV which unnecessarily substitutes 'preserve' in the last two verses.

3,4 The response. The encampment prepares for sleep. The sentries are placed, and, like the retreating king on the slopes of Jordan, the glad and confident exiles lie down to sleep (4.8).

5,6 *Who will stand on my right hand*
      To keep the bridge with me . . .?

asks Horatius in Macaulay's Roman poem. The companion on the swordarm side protected the warrior's exposed flank. His shield was on his left arm. The 'going-up' was not free from such military apprehensions.

Sun and moon are typical of two areas of danger. The sun in the desert is an ever-present foe, dehydrating the body and mercilessly pouring down its heat. The moon, in popular folklore, has always been associated with mental affliction – witness the word 'lunatic'. The statement is poetry and gives no countenance or sanction to imaginary dangers. The verse means simply to include mysterious and unseen perils.

7,8 In a word, the Lord's cover is comprehensive – body, soul, activity begun, activity concluded, and all between (see Deut. 28.6; 31.2; 1 Sam. 29.6 – and 1 Thess. 5.23).

Conclusion

This has been always a favourite psalm. It is worth learning by heart. There is always some high citadel of faith to which the eyes can be lifted. We do not 'keep the bridge' alone. All our doings are significant and under the eye of the Lord.

122

Read Psalm 122; Psalm 24

Occasion and author

The heading ascribes this psalm to David and traditional authorship, as has often been said in these studies, is not to be lightly disregarded. In this case, however, a few serious difficulties do arise. Most of the manuscripts of the Septuagint do not ascribe this piece to David, nor does the Latin Vulgate. Verse 5 contains a difficulty, but nothing there, or in the rest of the song, precludes the possibility that the song was a writing of David's last years when Jerusalem had become the place of worship which he envisaged, and a royal seat. Pilgrimage to Jerusalem did not require a temple for its significant functioning.

Commentary

1,2 Pilgrimage was not new to this writer. Jerusalem was of special significance to him. There is no need to believe that God is localized to feel a stirring of awe and reverence to stand in some place sanctified by holy feet. The Pavement below the Convent of the Sisters of Zion is such a place. The marks of the soldiers' gaming are sword-scratched on the floor. They include B for *Basileus*, a king, part of the crude fun of that hideous maltreatment. The kerb of a Roman road is visible where the rabbis stood, unable to go closer 'for fear of defilement'. Can a Christian fail to be moved? Pilgrimage still involves the thought that there are places where the aura of a presence makes it easier to comprehend. The feeling does not bear logical or theological analysis, nor does it need either. It is, none the less, a reality. So does this writer, David, or some other, feel about Jerusalem, already a full millennium old in Hebrew history.

3,4 Jerusalem confined between its deep ravines, a sort of acropolis in its own right, had to be compact ('bound firmly together', RSV; 'one united whole', JB; 'solid and unbroken', Moffatt). The shape of its eminence determined that, and in David's later years the place was packed with new buildings, a sight for the country tribesmen to see on the occasion of pilgrimage. Jeroboam, as a divisive policy, checked this practice.

5 It would in no way diminish the worth of the psalm if this verse were to be proved an insertion by the reverent editor of the psalms long after David's death. Jerusalem was the first civil metropolis (2 Sam. 5.9; 6.12,16).

6–9 The word 'peace' is embedded in the name of the city, and it is a tragic irony that war has so often afflicted the old stronghold. Jerusalem today is strangely pivotal in the power politics of the Middle East and the whole contending world.

Conclusion
The prayer of the closing four verses still holds and is still one for Christians to pray. If the threats which hang over Jerusalem are followed to their roots, and explored in all their ramifications, most of the menace which shadows the peace of humankind will be seen to be involved.

123

Read Psalm 123; Nehemiah 2

Occasion and author
Luther called this little psalm 'a deep sigh of a pained heart which looks around on all sides, and seeks friends, protectors and comforters and finds none'. He then looks with deep intensity to God, like a trained and eager servant who waits for no loud orders, but anticipates a wish or catches the merest sign of direction or command. Perhaps the writer was an exile, near the end of that ordeal, perhaps he was one of Nehemiah's despised Jews.

Commentary
1,2 The attitude of the servant may be documented from Latin literature. It was the slave's obligatory stance to maintain a watchful alertness. In the psalmist's phrase the suppliant thus waits with an 'eye of hope' on the movement of God's will. The times of Ezra and Nehemiah had a certain preoccupation with this figure of speech. 'The hand of God' was an expression for 'God in action' (Ezra 7.6,9,28; 8.18,22,31; Neh. 2.8,18).
3,4 The psalmist feels 'swamped with contempt' (Harrison). So the psalm ends – still in the dark, the prayer as yet unanswered, the suppliant still waiting. There is sometimes nothing else to do.

Conclusion
There is a sad little chorus in Aeschylus' *Agamemnon*, the greatest of the Greek dramas. It runs:

> *Zeus, whosoe'er indeed he be, –*
> *In that name, so it please him, hear.*
> *Zeus, for my help is none but he; –*
> *Conjecture through creation free*
> *I cast, and cannot find his peer,*
> *With this strange load upon my mind*
> *So burdening, only Zeus I find*
> *To life and fling it sheer.*

Catch the accent of man's ancient longing, which Abraham Lincoln put in simpler prose. "I have been driven many times to my knees by the overwhelming conviction that I had nowhere else to go. My own wisdom, and that of all about me seemed insufficient for the day.' It was such a refuge, in a God whom He called Father, that Christ gave to men.

124

Read Psalm 124; Psalm 69.1–16

Occasion and author

This is another occasion where the Davidic authorship is not fully attested. Three major manuscripts of the Septuagint and the Latin Vulgate do not refer to it. There are echoes of Davidic phrases (e.g. Pss. 28.6; 31.22), and it could be that the writer adopted a Davidic psalm to the present purpose – a triumph-song for the return from exile. Various commentators have conjectured that the poem is indeed part of David's experience, that it was written in celebration of Sennacherib's defeat and so on. If any of these conjectures were adopted, it would still remain certain that the psalm found a final place among the collected 'songs of ascent'.

Commentary

1–3 The peril is likened to the gaping earth of Korah's disaster. The same word is used in Num. 16.32,33.

4,5 Or perhaps like a torrent in a wadi, swollen to a raging flash flood by a cloudburst in the watershed – a not uncommon figure in a land where such a phenomenon was frequent (18.16; 69.1,2; 144.7; Isa. 8.7,8). 'Proudly-swelling' is a striking figure. Aeschylus, the Greek, quoted in the comments on the preceding psalm speaks of the 'arrogant river'.

6 Rushing on to another metaphor, the psalmist likens the peril to a wild beast, springing to rend . . .

7 Or yet to a bird, held in the net.

8 The theme of the opening verses is resumed. The 'name of the Lord' means 'the Lord in all His significance'. To 'believe in His name' (John 1.12) means 'to accept Him for all He said He was'.

125

Read Psalm 125; Nehemiah 6

Occasion and author

It is easy to see in this group of psalms the progression of phrase and idea linking psalm to psalm which was noticed in the first group – the Psalms of the Great Rebellion. Observe the preoccupation with the situation of Jerusalem. Zion was the fortified hill of pre-Israelite Jerusalem. Its meaning is not quite certain, but it probably signifies a hillcrest – which it is. The crag and its stronghold were called 'the city of David' after the events of 2 Sam. 5.6–10 and 1 Chron. 11.4–9. Numerous psalms seem to suggest that the name was extended to cover the Temple area (e.g. 84.5) and it is clear that in Maccabean times this geographical enlargement was common-place. In much of the Old Testament, Zion is equivalent to Jerusalem 51.18; Isa. 10.12). In similar poetic figure Zion becomes a synonym for the people of Jerusalem (97.8; Isa. 1.27; 33.5).

Commentary

1,2 Anyone who has climbed out of the deep valley to the summit of Zion, or has viewed the city from the Mount of Olives or some other of the surrounding eminences, will grasp the significance of the description. From almost any direction the pilgrim comes upon the city suddenly (he still does) over the summit of one of the sentinel hills. They are not high hills – Olivet is only 180 feet above Zion, but there are other eminences and raised country round about and further back, right to the mauve ridge of Moab.

3–5 The rod or sceptre may be the symbol of Persian rule, and though the exiles had returned, the land was not yet free. Perhaps the obscure expressions of this section refer to some sort of obstruction from Susa, and the infiltration of wickedness from surrounding satrapies which forms a tragic theme in Nehemiah's story.

126

Read Psalm 126; Revelation 22

Occasion and author

A restored exile wrote this pilgrim song and turned from an unutterable joy
to a prayer for aid in the task which immediately began. History does not
pause. Every ending is a new beginning.

Commentary

1–3 Those who came home to Zion had never seen the land of their fore-
fathers. Faithful fostering of the Word had kept alive the ancient memories
of the land, and the confidence that Israel was a land apart, with a unique
destiny, and that restoration was historically inevitable. It had come to
pass. Bishop Perowne quotes a similar moment in Roman history, as Livy
describes it in his vivid prose (33.32). The Macedonians had dominated
Greece destroying the institutions of the independent states until they
clashed with Rome who felt that her eastern approaches were menaced.
Rome won the war, and at the Isthmian Games in Corinth, Flamininus, to
the wondering incredulity of the Greeks, announced the restoration of
Greek liberty. The historian writes: 'The joy was too great for men to take it
all in. None could believe that he had heard aright, and they looked on one
another as though they were dreaming. And as though no one could believe
his own ears, each began questioning the person beside him.' So the Jews.

4–8 The South (the Negeb) is an arid, empty land. When the rains come it
can blossom. Life and green verdure flow back when the wadis fill. So with
the returning streams of men to make a desert of history fill with life again.
Then shall come some meaning for all the pain. Weeping, the long trains of
captives had gone to Babylon. They came home with some sense of purpose,
new life, God's overruling. The winter of their discontent was done, the
golden grain of reality was ready for their reaping.

127

Read Psalm 127; Proverbs 10

Occasion and author

'A psalm for Solomon,' runs the title (KJV). Perhaps it was 'by Solomon' and the gnomic tone would not be inappropriate. Why a fragment of 'wisdom literature' should be included in the 'songs of ascent' is not apparent. It is a picture of a settled community, not a pioneering one, a land not under immediate menace, much more in the spirit of Solomon's Golden Age that of the beleaguered Nehemiah.

Commentary

1 A man of mature years appears thus to reflect on life. He has seen the structures of man's materialism and selfish ambition crumble for all their carnal inventiveness.

2 The theme continues, as Harrison renders: 'It is a waste of time for you to get up early and go to bed late at night and eat hard-earned bread.' That is, as the sermon puts it, 'Take no anxious thought for the morrow . . .' 'The raven He feedeth, so why should I fear . . ?' Such quiet confidence is not easy to win, but who dare deny that it is the ideal and the final victory of faith? 'He gives sleep to his loved ones.'

That is, presumably, the quiet and trusting mind can relax and take its rest. The sequence of thought is not too clear, and so some have abandoned the beautiful KJV rendering, and take the words to mean that those who trust enough not to wear their lives away in struggling for a livelihood, find that God gives it while they rest peacefully. The corn grows and the barley sprouts for them as well as for the anxious.

3–5 The blessings of a family bound together in love and loyalty are an ancient and a lovely ideal. The psalm lingers over the picture. The man with a band of loyal sons is like a man with a quiver full of arrows. He faces the court in the city gate surrounded by them and feels confidence before the charges of his foes.

Conclusion

A wistful little picture in fact in a world where some fear to expose a family to the perils of a tense and violent age, or where family life has so eroded that pain lies where joy should dwell and the arrows in the quiver pierce the hand.

116

128

Read Psalm 128; Psalm 52

Occasion and author

Whoever wrote the last psalm surely also wrote this or found a model to imitate. It is another piece of wisdom literature, perhaps written with a lighter touch but revealing again a serenity hardly to be found in tense and ravaged times. The vine and the olive are familiar images, and as was shown in the comments on Psa. 52, the olive has given its branch as a symbol of peace, simply because it requires a long span of tranquillity for the oil-tree to come to fruition.

Commentary

1 The similarity to the first verse of the Psalter suggests a common authorship. Perhaps the man who put the psalms together, as was there suggested, attaining a serene tract of life back in his native land, wrote this piece as a marriage song or epithalamium.

2 See Lev. 26.6. The confidence of the writer is that war is not near, that peace has come. (See also Deut. 28.30–33, 39,40.)

3 A beautiful picture of stability and a home secure. It is part of the madness of today that such tranquillity is not held as life's ultimate blessing.

4 God in fact, has no more blessed gift to give on earth. 'Home is,' said a Roman proverb, 'where the heart is', and how true!

5 Of such homes nations are built. When such homes decay, and all that makes a home becomes the fodder of cheap wit, soiled minds, and dead hearts, a nation is doomed.

6 Doomed, for stability, continuity are gone.

Conclusion

Today the home is under sinister attack. Love is the butt of jeers, sex a cheap and grubby pastime. It is time for all who honour God to build in God's name (127.1), as never before, the Christian homes that will be the building bricks of revival, of permanence, of survival itself. This marriage-song is well sung if two lovers plight their troth in its words.

129

Read Psalm 129; Isaiah 51.21–52.2

Occasion and author

This small poem was written when the Captivity was a quivering memory of pain. It records conflict, persecution and final victory. The theme is God's righteousness. The writer (1) has shared the pain of his nation (2). He is back in Israel, in some country district.

Commentary

1 'Long have they . . .' The word is that of 120.6 and 123.4.
2 'And the darkness has not overcome it,' says John in a similar mood (John 1.5).
3 The poet was a countryman. Hence the rural imagery. Isaiah was a townsman. Compare his word-picture for the same cruel fate (51.23).
4 The cord which tied the captive to the alien plough (sustaining the rural image of the last verse), or the rope which bound the captive, has been slashed by the sword of God.
5,6 The grass on a housetop, its only nourishment the thin earth that collects in crevices and corners, withers with the first steady heat of the sun. A country dwelling was roofed with a plaster of mud and straw, and no doubt cleared when summer killed the intruding grass.
7 Such grass is worthless. It is of no use, not even for hay, mere weeds pulled up in a cleansing operation and thrown aside.
8 The countryman who wrote the words knew such scenes as those of Ruth 2.4. Perhaps he knew the Book of Ruth. The exchanged greeting of the relaxed reapers as the haywains went up and down is a fine touch of authenticity. The psalm ends with the writer's mind roving off down the paths of peace. Life was sweet at harvest time, and Babylon's great boulevards seemed far away. Life, thank God, has such islands of tranquillity and innocence.

130

Read Psalm 130; 1 John 1

Occasion and author

The writer has sinned. God is remote. The broken man lies in a pit of sorrow. Luther called this a 'Pauline Psalm', along with 32, 51 and 143. This psalm is also the sixth of the Penitential Psalms (6,32,38,51,106,130,143 is the list).

Commentary

1 From beneath waves and billows of pain, from the dark pit of agonizing self-consciousness, to a God who seems so far above that the uplifted arms cannot reach Him, the suppliant holds enough faith to cry aloud and expect an answer. There is no need to overdefine 'the depths', although commonly the figure applies to an overwhelming flood (40.2; 69.2,14). The dark experience of the psalmist is common enough among men who care for right and wrong, sin and struggle, for most readers to require no close definition.

2 'If out of the depths we cry,' says Maclaren, 'we shall cry ourselves out of the depths.' A gust of doubt sweeps across the suppliant's mind lest this fall short of truth. Will God hear? Can He hear?

3 But surely, he concludes, who does not need mercy? It is 'mercy all, immense and free' and confidence returns in the act of grasping this.

4 There is a definite article with the noun – 'the forgiveness'. This is not uncommon with many languages – Greek, for example, and French. But does the writer here mean, 'the forgiveness I need'? The noun itself seems to occur only in two other places – Neh. 9.17 and Dan. 9.9. A related verb is common enough. The word is not found in Hebrew before the days of the Exile, a hint, but only a hint, that the psalm is post-exilic. But what of the ending of the verse? God forgives, not as an indulgent father might or an equally fallible friend. 'He is faithful and just', not merely 'merciful', 'to forgive us our sins'. He forgives that we might the more deeply realize His nature. 'For thy name's sake, pardon my iniquities' (25.11) – 'because you are what you are, pardon me . . .'

5,6 The prosaic and theological explanations of this waiting, are prone to miss the deep psychological truth of these verses. The suppliant has claimed forgiveness and received it, but the truth takes time to penetrate heart and mind. There are wounds to heal, a convalescence from distress. There is a slow calming of the spirit as the tranquillity of God takes control, stills the recurring spasms of self-condemnation and heals the self-inflicted wounds. That man may be suspected of some lack of reverence, the 'fear of God' of

119

the Biblical phrase, who accepts God's grace like a package duly delivered to the outreached hand of faith. Faith does win forgiveness, repentance can claim it on the authority of God's word, but it is a sacred gift to be lifted with reverent and not casual hands. Hence the tarrying of these two verses.

7,8 The next movement of the forgiven soul is to desire that others should share the blessing. 'There is plenteous redemption, in the blood that has been shed . . .'

Footnote

Oscar Wilde's story of his fall and imprisonment takes its title from the first two words of this Psalm in the Vulgate – *De Profundis*, (Out of the Depths). It is an exquisite piece of writing, agonizingly sad. The brilliant, cynical wit, the man of polished letters, scholarship, urbanity, lays bare his shattered life. He nearly reaches Christ, he almost emerges from the pit of his despair . . . almost, but never finds Christ. It is infinitely sad, but a book to be read.

Read Psalm 131; Matthew 5.1–12

Occasion and author

There is no reason why the traditional ascription of the psalm should be rejected out of hand.

Commentary

1 Humility is the theme; the meekness of the Beatitudes. What is humility? It is the quality of love, which endures evil and does good.

Complete absence of pride is humility. The true Christian is a humble person. Humanity has done its worst with the word . . . ' "Oh, thank you, Master Copperfield," he answered, "I am sure it's very kind of you to make the offer, but I am much too 'umble to accept it." "What nonsense, Uriah." "Oh, indeed, you must excuse me, Master Copperfield. I am greatly obliged and I should like it of all things, I assure you, but I am far too 'umble. There are people enough to tread on me in my lowly state without my doing outrage to their feelings by possessing learning. A person like myself had better not aspire. If he is to get on in life, he must get on 'umbly, Master Copperfield." '

Is Uriah Heep, Dicken's satiric creation, the true type of the humble man? Surely not. Humility is not an abject, grovelling, self-despising spirit. It is a right estimate of ourselves. Christian grace humbles without degrading, and exalts without inflating. The first and surest test of all greatness, in scholarship, art, science, or any other human sphere is the absence of noisy self-assertion. It is the lesser man, seeking to pass for the greater, who must assert himself and behave unmannerly. Or to quote C. S. Lewis: 'Don't imagine that, if you meet a truly humble man, he will be what most people call "humble" nowadays; he won't be a sort of greasy, smarming person, who is always telling you that, of course, he is nobody. Probably all you'll think about him is that he seemed a cheerful, intelligent chap who took a real interest in what *you* said to *him* . . . He won't be thinking about humility; he won't be thinking about himself at all.' And to sum up with Chrysostom: 'Humility is the root, mother, nurse, foundation, and bond of all virtue.'

But is the psalmist losing humility by the very act of claiming it? No. This quiet prayer is a communication between a reverent soul and God. It is as though the reader listens in.

2 It is not a prayer of the Pharisee in the Temple. It is the quietness of the surrendered soul. Reverence, the very first element of religion, pervades it. Boyle, the pioneer physicist, it is said, never mentioned the name of God without a visible and reverent pause in what he was saying. Reverence, like its sister, humility, is strength not weakness. In quietness and confidence shall be a man's rest.

3 And he who so rests in God can wish that others so should do.

Conclusion

The RSV with its threefold repetition of the theme of tranquillity is a good rendering: 'But I have calmed and quieted my soul, like a child quieted on its mother's breast, like a child that is quieted is my soul.'

132

Read Psalm 132; 1 Kings 8.22–61

Occasion and author

Much conjecture surrounds the writing of this psalm. Some suggest that it was used on the occasion of the Ark's arrival on Zion, where a tabernacle was consecrated to house the sacred relic after its long sojourn in the country. Others, on the unsupported assumption that all the Pilgrim Songs were post-exilic, attribute it to the time of the consecration of the second Temple under Zerubbabel. The likeliest explanation is that it was a psalm of Solomon or written for Solomon, when he dedicated the temple he had built. It is natural that, at such a time, the earlier dwelling-place should be remembered, and the longing, never fulfilled, which David had, to house properly the symbols of God (2 Sam. 7.2).

Commentary

1,2 'O Lord, remember David in the time of his adversity . . .' It may, indeed, have been a thought of the desert night, in the days of exile and rejection – the thought that there was Another who 'had not where to lay His head'. A strong resolution could be looked upon as an oath.

3–5 Nor is there need to take literally such vows. This is a species of hyperbole to set in coloured thought the enduring determination not to forget the dominant ambition through all the common phases of life.

6 It is thus appropriate to remember how David had given himself to the first task, that of rescuing the sacred symbol from its long exile in Kirjath-jearim. Read: 'We heard of it in Bethlehem. We found it in the district of Jaar.' Ephrathah is Bethlehem, David's home town (Gen. 35.16,19; 48.7; Ruth 4.11; Micah 5.2). Jaar is another name for Kirjath-jearim (1 Sam. 7.1,2). 'Jaar' means a wood – hence the KJV rendering.

7 The resolve follows – to go to worship there. The place was God's place, though the home of His Ark was but a tent on a farmer's farm.

8 'Come up, O Lord, to your resting place', explains the purpose. At last the symbol of His presence was to go to a place prepared for it . . .

9 . . . with all due ceremony and priestly escort. Solomon's Temple stood gleaming above the choirs, but was it a greater day, says the king, than that on which his father, to a humbler Jerusalem, had brought the Ark home? There is a blending of past and present before the Eternal One.

10 For David's sake let David's son be accepted . . .

11,12 . . . for is not that a promise as sharp as the one fulfilled in the ceremony of the moment?

13,14 Look at 2 Sam. 24.18–25. The place was chosen as a sacred spot. All other places belonged to past history – Shiloh, Bethel (Judges 20.27), Mizpah (Judges 21.5), Kirjath-jearim . . .

15–18 There will David's power ('horn', 17) flourish and the royal priesthood serve with him. The metaphor of clothing appears twice (16,18). Clothes are part, a dominant part of the visual image which a person presents. They make the first impact in a watcher's or an observer's eyes. If the presence of a person turns the thoughts to a grace which that person ministers (16), to that person's degradation (18) – or indeed to Christ (Rom. 13.14) – it is natural to say that they are 'clothed' in that which they present.

Conclusion

There are moments in the life of a person or of a nation, when it is good to be alive, and when 'to be young is very heaven'. That it is why it is good to read this psalm. It set in verse and to music a high hour, and the song is properly included among the songs of pilgrimage because in days of stress and darkness it is healthy to remember the times of triumph and of sunshine. It is good always firmly to remember in the dark what God taught us in the light.

133,134

Read Psalms 133 and 134;
2 Samuel 1–5; 1 Chronicles
12.38–40

Occasion and author

This small lyric could be ascribed to the time when the land came to unity under David as king, a unity destined to bring a brief Golden Age of achievement and security. Disunity still plagues the world. It weakened the Greeks and denied that brilliant nation strength. Man has seldom known unity save when it is a unity in bondage, a unity enforced. It is a dream which extends from Isaiah's Servant Songs until today. Only a common faith can give it . . . Psalm 134 is simply a benediction closing the series of Pilgrim Songs, and addressed to the priests. Perhaps it was sung in greeting to the procession of worshippers who emerged singing in the courtyard.

Commentary

1 The key word is 'brethren'. Unity is possible only when men thus regard themselves, sons of a common father, and called to the love that brothers should hold.

2 The picture of the priestly figure, streaming with oil is not an attractive one to western minds. To the eastern mind, accustomed to the figurative use of the word oil for the rich blessing of the Spirit of God, it was a rich figure. The ancient world, right to the days of the Roman toga, must have more readily accepted oil on the garments than we do. The oil suggested frag-rance, for it was scented with frankincense, and plenitude of blessing, not soiling in any form.

3 This picture is much more acceptable to the westerner. Palestine's river, the historic Jordan, breaks out from the foothills of Hermon in three beauti-ful streams, gushing live from the rock which gave the Lord a word for Peter, and joining the equally pure little rivers, the Dan and the Hasbana to form the upper length of Jordan north of the Galilee lake. All three streams are fed by the snows of Hermon. So too among the mountains and hills of Judea, the dews, rains and winter snows fed any wadi stream that drained into the great rift valley.

Conclusion

Harmony, like the oil, like the springs of Hermon, must begin above and flow down. So the world's harmony. It begins in two hearts, permeates a family, flows outward to a community, and spreads through the world. And to one heart the force and benediction must begin by God's giving.

135,136

Read Psalms 135, 136

Occasion and author

This is one of a collection of Hallelujah Psalms separated from the rest of the group which fill the closing pages of the Psalter. It is placed thus out of sequence because it picks up and amplifies the theme of the preceding psalm – the exhortation to the priests and Levites. The theme is God in the nation's history, and His majesty over the 'un-gods' of the heathen.

The point to be noticed is that the psalm is almost completely composed of passages from other Old Testament sources, a species of mosaic, flowers, as Maclaren puts it, whose fragrance has long been loved and arranged now in a new bouquet. This is a common enough practice, and laudable too. Zephaniah takes words and phrases almost entirely from Jeremiah. Several psalms are composite. It has been observed that Pss. 97 and 98 are built out of the later chapters. The second of the two psalms practically repeats the former, adding only the repetitive refrain which turns it into a chant, and shifts the emphasis from praise to gratitude. Between those two words there is, to be sure, small distinction.

Commentary

135.1 See Pss. 134.1; 113.1.

2 See Psa. 134.1.

3 See Psa. 147.1.

4 See Exod. 19.5; Deut. 7.6.

5 See Exod. 19.5; 18.11.

6 (also 15–20) See Psa. 115 (whole).

7 See Jer. 10.13; Job 38.22

8–12 See Psa. 136. 10–22.

13–18 See Exod. 3.15; Deut. 32.36; Isa. 44.12–20; Jer. 10.6–10.

19,20 See Psa. 115.9–11.

21 See Pss. 128.5; 134.3.

136.1–26. The word 'kindness' is the nearest equivalent to the Hebrew *chesedh*. The beautiful word 'lovingkindness' is perhaps best. RSV 'steadfast love' is good, but 'covenant love' is too remote and cold.

Conclusion

First, let the richness of a mind stored with memories of God and great words about His goodness be observed. 'I store and lay aside that which shall stead me in aftertime,' said the Roman poet Horace of his philosophical studies.

A mind stored with great words, above all with scriptural sayings, is a mind to enjoy. There should be far more memorizing of Scripture.

Secondly, note again that which has been stressed before. The past can be a refuge and retreat from the tensions and terrors of the present. The mind can steady itself on memory.

Thirdly, note the blessedness of praise. Praise is an aid to prayer. He who most sharply bears in mind what God has done for him will the more readily ask for richer blessing.

> *When all Thy mercies, O my God,*
> *My rising soul surveys,*
> *Transported with the view, I'm lost*
> *In wonder, love and praise.*

Read Psalm 137; Romans 12

Occasion and author

A returned exile with the wrongs of the captivity in Babylon hot upon his heart wrote this little drama. Observe the word. To understand any piece of literature, the type of literature to which it belongs must first be identified. No one would go to *Macbeth* for Scottish history, historical though the play is, nor to *Coriolanus* for Roman history, realistic though the treatment of the division in the Republic is in that powerful tragedy.

If this piece is taken as drama, a setting-down in poetic form of some dreadful hour of suffering by the Euphrates, then it makes sense. The gentle, sad beginning shows the shattered exiles meeting, as exiles did, under the Euphrates willows. It was their formal meeting, for thus, by riversides, the Jews of the Dispersion who had no synagogue were ever wont to meet (cf. Acts 16.13). The fierce words with which the psalm ends are a quotation from the commination which was the only defence of the persecuted. It is evident from the opening verses that aliens gathered round asking for a song. It was a menacing situation, and the captives had no means of warding off the dangerous crowd save by, in solemn terms, invoking on Babylon the very horrors which they themselves had seen and suffered on the cobbled lanes of Jerusalem. The psalm is a dramatic episode.

This leaves to be discussed the nature of the 'commination' – a form which survives still in the Anglican prayer book. The exiles, pressed hard by the cruel, demanding crowd by the river, had only one hope of safety – to overwhelm the mob psychologically. The curse in ancient times meant much more than it does today. A formal curse was a potent and a legitimate weapon. Dr. C. T. Cook quotes a telling example (*The Christian*, Nov. 19, 1965). 'During the nineteenth century,' he writes, 'a distinguished Cambridge scholar, Professor E. H. Palmer, who had specialized in Oriental studies, was engaged in a survey of Sinai, during which he acquired a marvellous knowledge of the wild Arab tribes. A man of many parts, he was for a time Professor of Arabic at Cambridge. In 1822, on the eve of Arabi Pasha's rebellion in Egypt, Dr. Palmer was given by the British Government the perilous mission of winning over the Sinai tribes to Britain . . . He and his companions were murdered by the Arabs. It was reported that just before he was killed Palmer solemnly cursed his murderers.'

Dr. Cook proceeds to quote Sir Walter Besant's illuminating comment on this grim event. 'Some of Palmer's friends have been pained to think that his last moments should have been spent in cursing his enemies. It must, however, be understood that cursing, in the hands of an Oriental who understands how to curse, is a most powerful weapon of defence. Palmer knew every form of Arab cursing. He was driven to do this as his last resource. If he could not deter them by cursing, he could do no more. And again, to understand an Oriental curse, one must go back to the Old Testament. Such a curse is a solemn and an awful thing. It falls upon a man and weighs him down and crushes him; it brings with it a fearful foreboding of judgement; it lies like lead upon a guilty heart; it helps to bring the crime to light and the criminals to justice. I have no doubt whatever that the denunciations of woe, ruin, desolation and death – Palmer's last words – which fell upon the ears of those wild desert men, and were echoed back from the rocks around them, became to them a prophecy, sure and certain as the vengeance of the Lord.'

This in no way contradicts Paul's precept written to the Roman Christians centuries later (Rom. 12.14). The 'exiles' in Rome felt equally despised and hurt. The 'great Babylon' of the New Testament was the capital of the harsh persecutor. The new name of historic condemnation which haunts the Apocalypse was already current speech. No doubt ancient curses rose to Jewish Christian lips, not wild and meaningless, but words which were shields and weapons. Paul bids them, like Christ, to forswear such aid and such assuagement for the soul.

Commentary

1,2 The vast monotonous plain, where the great city stood by the Euphrates, willow-lined, amid the intersecting complex of irrigation canals, could hardly differ more from Jerusalem's rocky ridge. Here was the beginning of the synagogue, the great creation of the Dispersion, the future stepping-stone for Christianity.

3 The sinister crowd has gathered, perhaps at the sound of a Jewish lament. They call for a merry song, but the Jews, their privacy and worship violated, have hung their harps on the willows and sit with downcast eyes. They have learned from returning soldiery of Jerusalem and Zion, but such words sound harsh on alien lips.

4 Hence the retort perhaps not put into words until the time of writing, as the poet seeks to wash an evil memory from his mind.

5,6 He is home now and in a passion of love looks at the hills of home, shattered though their crowning ring of walls may still have been.

7 His circling eye looking east from Zion sees the blue line of the hills of Moab, where Ishmael, the ancient enemy lived, as he lives today. The Edomites had laughed at Jerusalem's downfall.

8,9 Then the writer returns to the well-remembered day by the willow-lined river. Thus had the little band of menaced folk daunted and dispersed their foe. Remember too, that they had seen the bloody hands of Babylon's soldiery dash the life from their children. It is easy to forget the blazing pain of others, and to condemn hot words when the occasion has never been part of the cool critic's experience. Does this interfere with any doctrine of inspiration? Not at all. This cameo drama is a document of truth. It shows what happened and is set down as God permitted, not to form a theme for condemnation of those who suffered beyond human bearing, but to show what pain can do to the spirit of man.

Conclusion

Let it be noted that Babylon today is a desert waste, a ruin heap where the archaeologist probes and trenches for the fragmented relics of a vanished empire. Jerusalem, old and new, spreads, alive and vital, though, alas, not yet Christian, over hill and ridge.

Footnote

Winifred Walker believes (*All the Plants of the Bible*, 1958, p. 232) that the willows of the psalm were the Euphrates aspen, found along the banks of rivers in a wide area of the Middle East. 'The tree,' she says, 'grows as high as forty-five feet. Its crisp leaves are borne on flattened stems and attached obliquely to the main stalk. This causes them to droop and hang down and continually sway back and forth, like "weeping and wailing women". These leaves are only one and a half inches long and heart-shaped; in the early spring little green catkins appear among them. According to one legend, this aspen furnished the wood for Jesus' cross, so that ever since, the leaves of all aspen trees have quivered and trembled.' The botanical name is *populus euphratica*.

On the other hand the riverside tree known popularly as the 'weeping willow' has the botanical name of *salix babylonica*, or Babylon willow.

Both *populus euphratica* and *salix babylonica* are called by the Arabs *'arabim*. So the puzzle remains – fascinating but quite irrelevant to our understanding of this poignant poem.

138

Read Psalm 138; Philippians 1

Occasion and author

There is no reason to discard the traditional authorship, although it is fair to add that the Septuagint adds also the names of Haggai and Zephaniah. A more pertinent matter for discussion is why eight psalms attributed to David are inserted at this point in the Psalter. They are typical Davidic psalms, personal, haunted by strain, tension and the power of temptation, as well as with gladness. The editor of the psalms may have felt the need, among the less personal hymns of the smaller collections out of which he built this book, to return to the type of song which dominated the earlier books. A collection of David's psalms, perhaps temporarily set aside, or perhaps recently come to light, offered this facility.

Commentary

1 The 'gods' were quite simply the gods of surrounding heathendom. David by no means grants them life, power, or reality. We too easily take monotheism for granted. In days of defeat and apparent rejection it was easy to be gripped by a cold fear lest there were powers at large, worshipped in bloody and obscene rituals, which could prove more powerful than the Hebrew God. It is significant that the plagues of Egypt struck at the spheres and powers of things deified by the Egyptians. In a moment of panic, fear and disillusionment, Israel made a golden calf, a Hebrew Apis to represent their silent God. And can anyone claim never to have been brushed in thought by some gust of doubt or apprehension lest some loud and arrogant system of thought might after all be truth? David, in a moment of fulfilment and victory, found such fear fall away.

2 Other versions clear up the difficulty caught in the KJV translation: '. . . for thou hast exalted above everything thy name and thy word' (RSV). The Septuagint felt the difficulty and rendered: 'thou hast magnified thy holy name above all.' If, however, the phrase is taken as the KJV translates it, there is no difficulty save that created by western logic in dealing with eastern hyperbole. It is true that 'the name of God cannot be surpassed by any individual act or attribute of God, for every such separate act is a manifestation of that name . . .' (Hupfeld). But all the psalmist means is, as Perowne puts it, that 'the promise becomes so precious, so strong a ground of hope, that it surpasses all other manifestations of God's goodness and truth . . .'

3 The NEB catches the power of this verse well: '. . . thou didst answer me and make me bold and valiant-hearted.' Courage in the core of the being expresses itself in thought, word and action. 'Strength in the soul,' as one translator renders it, is what we need, what we need indeed.

4 The evangelical ambition in these words is an occasional flash from the pages of the Old Testament.

5 It was, in fact, an ambition of more enlightened Jewry in quite early days. Perowne quotes Ibn Ezra: 'They shall no more sing of love or war, but of the glory of the Lord.' It was the old vision of Isaiah, for which the world still yearns.

6 There is no difficulty in the text as the KJV renders it. The proud can never be near God, though they do not escape His watchful eye. Iniquities divide between man and God, and the basic sin of all sin, arrogance, self-exaltation, makes an effective barrier which cannot be crossed.

7 David had said as much in Psa. 23 – or was to say it, for this psalm cannot be effectively linked to any set of circumstances.

8 'The Lord will fulfil His purpose for me . . .' This is certainty – Paul had the verse in mind when he wrote to the Philippian church (1.6).

Conclusion
It is easy to see why this psalm should have a peculiar appeal after the return from exile. God sometimes speaks to the soul by suddenly illuminating something, some word, verse or incident, long known but freshly realized. The place of this prayer in the midst of a largely post-exilic collection is thus explained.

Read Psalm 139; Romans 11

Occasion and author
This is one of the most magnificent of the psalms, memorable for its comprehension of the omniscience, the love, almost the relentless love, of God pursuing the sinner to the very last nooks and crevices of his timid hiding-place. This psalm, one might imagine, gave Francis Thompson the idea for his fine poem *The Hound of Heaven*. It should be read. With that touch of uncertainty which haunted the ascription of these psalms, the Septuagint gives Psa. 139 to Zechariah, but there is no reason to reject the Davidic tradition. Some Aramaic colouring of language could have a simple explanation quite consonant with the tradition of origin.

Commentary
1–4 God, as Paul says, is not mocked. It is final folly to imagine that the moral law which is interwoven with the whole sum of things can be flouted

any more than man can disregard the law of gravity. 'As sure as water will wet us, as sure as fire will burn,' as Kipling put it in his *Gods of the Copy Book Headings*, so an all-knowing God will perceive, understand, bless, guide, udge. Prayer has for one of its functions the practice of utter honesty, searching self-revelation, complete humility (Rom. 11.33).

5–12 There is no escape from God. He pursues the sinner. He finds the guilty. No man is lost save he who, determined in his flight, outdistances the following feet of God. This was Francis Thompson's point:

> *I fled Him, down the nights and down the days;*
> *I fled Him, down the arches of the years;*
> *I fled Him, down the labyrinthine ways*
> *Of my own mind; and in the mist of tears*
> *I hid from Him, and under running laughter.*
> *Up visitaed hopes I sped;*
> *And shot, precipitated,*
> *Adown Titanic glooms of chasmèd fears,*
> *From those strong Feet that followed, followed after.*
> *But with unhurrying chase,*
> *And unperturbèd pace,*
> *Deliberate speed, majestic instancy*
> *They beat – and a Voice beat*
> *More instant than the Feet –*
> *'All things betray thee, who betrayest Me.'*

Verse 9 means 'from east to west'. The wings of the morning are often visible when the sun, just below the horizon flings up a fan of light. It would be a common phenomenon above the purple ridge of the mountains of Moab. The sea, of course, bounded all the west.

It is human folly to seek to escape from God. His hands hold, as His crook restrains (Psa. 23.4).

13–16 And who can know us better than He who was the author of the wondrous process by which our living, sensate selves were separated.

Verse Fourteen is quite adequately rendered in the KVJ. The RSV follows unnecessarily the Septuagint. Wonder, said Plato, is the beginning of philosophy. It is the beginning, too, of worship. To see the wonder of Creation is the first step in the quest for its author. Man alone, a God-conscious being, loses a dimension of his humanity when he ceases to wonder. Observe that God is interested in the unborn child, a point which necessarily determines the Christian attitude towards abortion. The embryo is His work, and the subject of love and interest of One who sees future potential and value in the first beginnings of life.

17,18 The old classic of Brother Lawrence, three centuries old, finds exquisite illustration here. The sense of an awaiting presence greets the first waking thought. God has been there 'all through the night' (Psa. 4.8).

19–22 The sudden outburst against evil has a ready psychological explanation. Derek Kidner comments well:

'The very clarity of the vision makes the anomaly of evil, boasting in full view of God, intolerable; so David's re-entry to the atmosphere of earth creates, as we might say, a sudden incandescence. The abrupt change in the psalm from reverie to resolve is disturbing, but wholly biblical in its realism; and the last two verses emphasize the continuity of this stanza with what has gone before, transposing the truths of the opening verses into the key of willing acceptance and surrender.

For all its vehemence, the hatred in this passage is not spite, but zeal for God. In the "day of salvation" the New Testament will re-direct this fighting spirit, but it will endorse its single-mindedness ("What fellowship has light with darkness? What accord has Christ with Belial?")'

23,24 'That man must have a rare confidence,' said Calvin truly, 'who offers himself so boldly to God's scrutiny.' And yet this is a duty of prayer if John 3.19–21 is part of the Christian's path to victory. If we cannot face in humility this bold self-revelation there is something awry, and here Calvin betrays some misunderstanding. Let, then, our prayer be:

> *Search me, O God! my actions try,*
> *And let my life appear*
> *As seen by Thine all-searching eye –*
> *To mine my ways make clear.*
>
> *Search all my sense, and know my heart,*
> *Who only canst make known,*
> *And let the deep, the hidden part*
> *To me be fully shown.*
>
> *Search all my thoughts, the secret springs,*
> *The motives that control;*
> *The chambers where polluted things*
> *Hold empire o'er the soul.*
>
> *Search, till Thy fiery glance has cast*
> *Its holy light through all,*
> *And I by grace am brought at last*
> *Before Thy face to fall.*

140

Read Psalm 140; Romans 3

Occasion and author

The only objections of any weight against the Davidic authorship of this psalm are one or two words found nowhere else. The phenomenon could be accounted for by supposing a few touches of Levitical adaptation to the language patterns of a later age – a supposition in no way calculated to diminish the authority of the psalm.

The theme is one not uncommon in David's psalms, a loathing of violence, slander and treachery.

Commentary

1 The prayer is one which is increasingly relevant in the modern world. 'Nothing good,' said Luther, 'ever came out of violence', and the words might be borne in mind, not only by abandoned men with whom violence is a way of life, but by quasi-religious groups who condone violence in the name of freedom. Violence is damnable whenever it rears its head, in whatever cause, and by whoever it is exercised.

2 To plot and plan violence is one step more detestable than employing it in a moment of passion. Such men are 'of their father the devil' (John 8.34–47).

3 'Slander,' said Samuel Johnson, 'is the revenge of the coward, and dissimulation his defence.' The slanderer and the murderer differ only in their weapons.

4 The second strophe picks up artistically the opening theme of the first, '. . . they plan to trip up my feet.'

5 The arrogant, the self-confident are the natural products of godlessness. They are equally the natural, and sometimes the dedicated, enemies of godliness and good.

6 The shield and buckler – prayer.

7 The helmet – God's shadowing hand.

8 'Do not allow the desires of the wicked to be realized, Lord; do not let their plans succeed' (Harrison).

9 There is nothing wrong in the prayer that deliberate evil will return to its place of origin, recoil on the head of its inventor.

10 Fire and water, two elemental forces according to the speculations of the Ionian philosophers. Some primitive law in the whole structure of the universe ultimately punishes evil. Perhaps the poet of the psalm reaches for some such truth. The forces of nature are in the end ranged against the wicked.

11 The forces which an evil man lets loose ultimately turn and destroy him. 'Let evil hunt down the violent man speedily' (RSV).
12,13 The quiet ending follows the storm. In the end good will prevail: 'Make haste, O Lord, to save us.'

141

Read Psalm 141

Occasion and author

The psalm could come from the days of the Great Rebellion, when, in retreat from Absalom, David was cut off from the place of prayer and formal worship (2).

Commentary

1 The opening is a common one in David's psalms. He has no difficulty in assuming naturally, that, when the accoutrements and accompaniments of worship are lacking, the lifting of the hands in prayer can stand for incense and for sacrifice (Exod. 29.38–42; Lev. 2.1–11; Num. 28.3–8). 'Let my prayer be counted as incense before thee, and the lifting up of my hands as an evening sacrifice' (RSV).
3,4 David was well aware of the place where evil had its roots and genesis. He had said as much in the most agonized of the psalms (51.6,10). He would have the very impulse to do wrong quenched in the deep core of the personality (Luke 6.45). Nor would he be accepted at their table.

C. S. Lewis' penetrating essay the *Inner Ring* comes to mind.

Lewis took as his text a paragraph from Tolstoy's *War and Peace*. Prince Andrey was receiving a report from a senior general when Boris entered. Andrey, a mere captain in the army, turned from the general and greeted the lieutenant with outstretched hand.

With a glow of delight Boris saw what he had long suspected – that alongside the army's system of subordination was another system which, in effect, gave a subaltern of the proper colour precedence over a general. He was accepted, and determined that the privilege should endure.

Such is 'the Inner Ring', a hierarchy not formally constituted, elusive, a reality never confessed. It shares certain standards which can too readily fall short of complete integrity. It has its passwords. It tends to invade and dominate essential executives. It is no prerogative of any party, group or calling, but it is a fact of which a free man should be aware.

The price of acceptance, emolument, advantage, can be high, even in the natural quest for some form of promotion, but what Lewis had princip-

133

ally in mind was the less tangible, less reputable groupings of life. 'Over a cup of coffee or a drink,' he said, 'disguised as a triviality, from the lips of someone you hope to know better – just when you are most anxious not to appear crude or naïve – the hint will come. It is about something which is not quite in accordance with the rules of fair play. The cup is so near your lips that you cannot bear to be thrust back. And then, if you are drawn in, it will be something a little further from the rules – all in the friendliest spirit. It may end in a crash, a scandal. It may end in millions and giving out the prizes at your old school, but you will be a scoundrel.'

Beware, then, the price. If it is servility to some Prince Andrey, lift up your head and walk out. The cost may be a cherished object but as One said who suffered at the hands of the Inner Ring, 'a man can gain the world and lose his soul.'

David has some such thought in mind. Integrity can be lost in too great a fellowship with evil.

5 Just reproach he will accept: 'May I never be too proud to accept it' (Harrison).

6 'They shall founder on the rock of justice; they shall learn how acceptable my words are' (NEB). This seems the best that can be made of this difficult verse. The three verses in this section (5–7), in fact, constitute the difficulty of this psalm. They are abrupt, lack coherence each with the others, and could be a case of some ancient and irremediable corruption in the text. The best that can be made of the sequence is that the judges of his enemies, part of the context of confronting evil, will themselves be judged, vindicating his (David's) words.

7 There is an ancient conflict of readings, 'our bones', followed by the KJV and others, and 'their bones' (RSV, NEB). The former would be a sort of cameo, an outburst on his state or that of the nation, to be fragmentarily compared with Ezekiel's vision of the shattered remnants of Israel (Ezek. 37.1–14). The second reading, giving the NEB rendering ('Their bones shall be scattered at the mouth of Sheol, like splinters of wood or stone on the ground') would continue vividly the violent metaphor of the fallen false judges. But all three verses are admittedly difficult to explain and integrate.

8–10 'For . . .' continues the difficulty. It seems to refer to the plea at the beginning of the psalm, to vs. 4,5. Hence the 'but' with which the KJV, avoiding the difficulty, opens the verse. The answer to the trials of life, he is saying, is to turn the eyes steadfastly to God. The image, like that of the refuge is common in the Davidic psalms. In v. 9 'from the hands of the snares' is the literal translation, as though evil were so many clutching hands. That is how it sometimes feels. So (literally) 22.20,21: 'from the hand of the dog', and Isa. 47.14 – 'from the hand of the flame.' And the simple triumph of the conclusion is, as Kidner renders it: 'While as for me, I pass right on.'

Conclusion

Ideally, that is how it should be. The psalm is a sort of pilgrimage, a journey through the valley of the shadow:

Where startled faces flicker in the gloom
And horrid whispers set the cheek aghast . . .

and where clutching hands of treachery reach, pluck, cling. But 'as for me, I pass right on . . .'

Such is the consummation to be grasped in courageous faith:

Be swift, my soul, to follow Him,
Be jubilant, my feet.

Read Psalm 142; Psalm 57; 1 Samuel 22.1,2

Occasion and author

The traditional ascription leaves no doubt of either. This is the last of a series of eight psalms which arise from the times of Saul's pursuit and persecution. How it came, like the next psalm, to be dissociated from others of like background and character, cannot be said. A storm of ruin had, however, swept across the land, and like the Renaissance scholars of Florence and Rome, delightedly discovering new manuscripts of Greek and Latin authors in forgotten monastery libraries, it is not at all impossible that the post-exilic editor was continually finding documents of the past or discovering someone who retained the verbal memory of great prayers and songs. The mood differs from the companion piece. Psalm 57 contains a note of jubilation and strength. In this psalm such a mood has vanished. But is not that precisely what happens? The trough follows the peak of the wave.

Commentary

1,2 'Out of the depths I cry to Thee' . . . the depths are real, but the wondrous truth about faith is that the soul which is lost in them knows to whom to cry. On Psa. 130, the book *De Profundis* (Out of the Depths) of Oscar Wilde was mentioned. Poor Wilde suffered the agonies of the depths – but knew not to whom to lift his voice. Harrison renders: 'I empty myself of grief in his presence, and tell him of my trouble' (2). There is only one place, in blessed fact to empty out one's grief.

3,4 'When my spirit darkens within me', the verse runs. There are dark hours of the soul when the night seems to invade the mind and heart, but not if God knows the path. On December 25, 1939, George VI in his slow, earnest voice quoted Minnie Louise Haskens: 'I said to the man who stood at the gate of the year: "Give me a light that I may tread safely into the unknown." And he replied: "Go out into the darkness and put your hand into the hand of God. That shall be to you better than light, and safer than a known way." ' It is worth quoting again. 'Who will stand on my right hand and keep the bridge with me?' asked Macaulay's Horatius. The friend guarded the sword-arm as was mentioned above. David, in a gust of despair, cannot see God there.

5–7 'To thee, Lord, I cry, claiming thee for my only refuge, all that is left me in this world of living men' (5, Knox). 'Pursuers' is the better word in v. 6. 'Persecutors', of course, is basically the same word. One comes from Latin through French, the other more directly from the original. But meanings have diverged, and David was never free from his preoccupation, the sound of feet behind him, the cry of the pack in pursuit. There is a sense of confinement, a hemming in, a claustrophobia which stifled joy, freedom, abandonment in worship.

Conclusion
The same cave can be a refuge (5) and a prison (7). Such is the pattern of life as we colour the same scene with the hues of jubilation or distress. It is well steadily to remember the fact, for it leads to the point where recovery lies and healing of the vision must begin.

Read Psalm 143 and Psalm 51

Occasion and author
The remarks on the last psalm apply. Perhaps it is a companion piece to the most agonized of all the psalms, that of David's deep repentance. A few copies of the Septuagint ascribe it to the time of Absalom's rebellion. It is the seventh and last of the penitential psalms.

Commentary
1 It is God's faithfulness and righteousness that are the basis of the plea. Who can stand without the complete integrity of the judge?

2 At the same time, the psalmist continues, 'pulled up short', as Derek Kidner perceptively remarks, 'by the word he has used', let God not 'put His servant on trial' (Moffatt and JB), for who can stand when He appears? Only the cross, as has already been remarked, resolved the problem of justice and grace (1 John 1.9).

3,4 Every word is loaded with distress. Look reverently at Matt. 26.38,39 and realize afresh, as far as the human mind is capable of such a reach of understanding, what the Lord also suffered. Wondrous it is in days of sorrow, to know that He suffered as we do (Heb. 4.15,16).

5 A familiar refuge. 'I dwell upon the years long past, upon the memory of all that thou hast done; the wonders of Thy creation fill my mind' (NEB).

136

6 Therefore, like the arid desert, burned, baked and bared by a merciless summer sun, his dry soul is ready to soak up the downpour. A passage of Lewis' *Screwtape Letters* comes to mind. Lewis, in the imaginary correspondence of the senior demon, describes how God seeks to promote maturity. He writes: 'Sooner or later He withdraws, if not in fact, at least from their conscious experience, all those supports and incentives. He leaves the creature to stand up on its own legs – to carry out from the will alone duties which have lost all relish. It is during such trough periods, much more than during the peak periods, that it is growing into the sort of creature He wants it to be. Hence the prayers offered in the state of dryness are those which please Him best.' Such is this prayer.

7–12 At this point the psalm becomes a tissue of quotations from earlier psalms. There are seven quotations in v. 7 alone. Perhaps the suppliant in the stress and pain of his mind cannot phrase his prayers but falls back on the language of earlier days. There is no reason why a numbed and harassed spirit should not thus take refuge in the past and spare his battered mind all strain of thinking. This may be the reason. Or it could be that the first half of the psalm was recovered intact, and the editor expanded it by a catena of passages relevant to the theme rebuilding the broken parts into a new and coherent whole.

Verse 10 says literally 'on to level ground'. The term is used of the plain which fell to Reuben's inheritance (Deut. 4.43). Level land is easier on the feet. If the 'crooked is made straight and the rough places plain', the path is easier to find and smoother for weary feet to walk upon.

Conclusion

Let a further paragraph from the *Screwtape Letters* conclude and sum up the theme: 'Do not be deceived, Wormwood. Our cause is never more in danger than when a human, no longer desiring, but still intending, to do our Enemy's will, looks round upon a universe from which every trace of Him seems to have vanished, and asks why he has been forsaken, and still obeys.'

144

Read Psalm 144; Psalm 18

Occasion and author

This is another Davidic anthology added to a clearly original portion. All are fragments of authoritative and authentic origin.

Commentary

1–11 The whole section has been examined in other contexts. The likeliest explanation is that David drew material from earlier composition in order to express the mood of the moment, or else sections of David's writing could have been placed in a new arrangement for liturgical use.

12–15 An abrupt contrast closes the psalm. This indeed may point to the purpose of the eleven preceding verses. They began with storm and peril and passed into prayer. The prayer is consummated in the idyll of a land at peace. The similes of v. 12 are beautiful. The sons have the green strength of vigorous young trees, the daughters are pictured as 'sculptured pillars at the corners of a palace' (NEB). The Caryatids, supporting in polished dignity the porch on the Erechtheum, come to mind. Harrison's rendering of the last half of v. 14 touches a modern note . . . 'that there be no disturbances in our city streets'. It is all a beautiful picture of a balanced community, based on agriculture, with peaceful and elegant towns. It touches a note of longing in the mind of this city-ridden age.

145

Read Psalm 145; John 1.1–18

Occasion and author

This is the last of the alphabetical psalms. It had a special place in the old
Jewish services, and in Christian worship is regarded as appropriate for
Whitsunday. Davidic authorship is again traditional but this could mean
that it was built by a later writer out of Davidic material. The theme, like
that of many of these closing psalms, is 'for Thine is the Kingdom and the
Power and the Glory . . .' In the alphabetical arrangement the letter (N)
(Nun) is missing. The Septuagint tried to fill the gap without much originality. A Qumran fragment supplies the missing verse, which the RSV puts
at the end of v. 13 as also the Jerusalem Bible. In the NEB it starts v. 14.

Commentary

1–3 A contribution to religious thought unique to the Hebrew people is
the realization that God's greatness is 'unsearchable' ('unfathomable', NEB).
Revelation, however did not stop there, and it is here where those who halt
short of the New Testament stumble. David Hume was right, two centuries
ago, when he pointed out that the gap between the small agitation in the
brain which we call thought, and the measureless Intelligence which
Christians call God, is so enormous, that what one concludes about the other
has little significance. Correct, but for the vital core of Christian belief.
Christ revealed God in terms understandable to man.

That is where the glory of God is finally revealed.

4–7 With some glimpse of a progressive revelation, the psalmist sees the
continuity of God in history, each making a contribution to posterity, as
generations past have added to what he knows and understands. Majesty,
wonder, terror, merging into goodness and righteousness are the notes
struck. 'Grace and truth came with Jesus Christ.'

8,9 And yet there is an inkling of truth as old as Moses (Exod. 34.6) which
touches the edge of the vast compassion to be shown in full truth in the
Incarnate Son. These verses are deeply evangelical.

10–12 The theme returns to history and the visible manifestation of 'something far more deeply interfused', which is a preoccupation of Book Five.

13 The everlasting kingdom is a similar preoccupation. In Babylon, exiled
Jewry had learned that world empire is a fragile thing.

14 And yet what use is imperial power unless it filters through to the
lowliest citizen . . .

15 . . . and unless the royal monarch has an ear for the humble . . .

139

16 . . . and satisfies the needy?

17 And such is the Lord. 'All' His ways, 'all' His works include those worked out in the smallest parts of His Kingdom.

18,19 He is not far removed in citadel and palace but in street and market place – 'near to those who call', attentive to their cry like Christ hearing Jericho's blind Bartimaeus through the crowd's din.

20,21 As though to conclude David's final contribution to the Psalter comes a testimony (20) and a doxology. With this we bid farewell to a great man, noble but faulty, sinning greatly, but greatly penitent, royal and faithful, afflicted and wrestling with doubt, but ending, where so many who are too humanly like him trust they too may end, recognizing a great hand over their life and praising Him for ever and ever.

Read Psalm 146; 2 Timothy 4.16–22

Occasion and author

The Psalter closes with some hymns of worship. Ralph Venning, the nonconformist divine of three centuries ago said something pertinent to these psalms: 'The tongue blessing God without the heart is but a tinkling cymbal; the heart blessing God without the tongue is sweet but still music; both in concert make their harmony, which fills and delights heaven and earth.' The courts of the old Temple must have been loud with the music of the psalms, something appearing for the first time in history and filling the whole of the echoing pile of hills where Jerusalem stands. The Hallelujah Psalms are anonymous, though the Septuagint preserves two traditions, variously assigning this hymn to Haggai and Zechariah.

Commentary

1,2 A call to worship, a command in the plural, and then a personal resolve: 'I mean to praise God all my life. I mean to sing to my God as long as I live' (Jerusalem Bible). It is for the sake of man, not of God that praise and worship are devised. Such uplifting of the mind solemnizes the heart, diminishes self, and sanctifies.

3 Anyone who has known the broken promises, the forgotten pledges, the disloyalty, mendacity and faithlessness of men, who has vainly relied on undertakings to aid, to support and promote, can echo the sentiment of this verse.

4 There is a wordplay in the Hebrew on the words for 'man' and 'earth' which are almost identical. It is as though the writer said: 'Why, indeed, should one ever rely upon this thing of clay, this walking shadow which struts for its brief season and is gone?'

5–10 The last Beatitude of the psalms is an extended benediction with the beat of the Levites' music echoing round the city, fixing at every phrase something vital in the mind.

Read Psalm 147; Isaiah 40.1–5

Occasion and author

One might imagine this to be a song of encouragement written in the days of Nehemiah when the city was at last taking shape, the first crops springing in soil long fallow, and some confidence returning to the embattled repatriates.

Commentary

1,2 There was one supreme moment in ancient history when God called home the exiles of Israel. Verse 2 surely dates the psalm. In Israel's modern history this verse can hardly do other than stir the soul.

3 In the first suffering of those who struggled home this truth needed reinforcing. Some had left loved ones behind in a hot surge of devotion which had chilled in the harsh winds of hardship.

4,5 A God so infinite must also understand, must be good, and therefore must, in the end, show the meaning of that which He permits.

6 Even in the brief span of the exiles' experience, they had seen this happen; great Babylon down, and Sanballat frustrated.

7,8 The harvest, too, was home, and the basic anxiety of a pioneer community lifted.

9 Even the dark raven, the unclean bird, was not disregarded. In his embracing faith the psalmist sees God's power outpoured in all the channels of creation. As the old evangelistic hymn put it:

> *In tender compassion and wonderful love,*
> *The Father looks down from on high;*
> *He knoweth the raven hath need of its food,*
> *And heareth in mercy its cry.*

> *The raven He feedeth, then why should I fear?*
> *To the heart of the Father His children are dear;*
> *So, if the way darkens or storms gather o'er,*
> *I'll simply look upward and trust Him the more.*

10 And what are the strutting empires with chariotry, cavalry, and long, long files of marching robots, 'boots, boots, boots, boots, going up and down again', to Him? 'The strength of the warhorse means nothing to Him, it is not infantry that interests Him'.

11 It is spiritual values which ultimately prevail and that is true in history. No nation has yet fallen by assault from without which has not first destroyed itself within.

12–18 And it is the same Hand seen in the walls rising course by course of heavy stone, the gates of Zion sturdily barred, and the distant waving fields of wheat, the snows, the hail, the winds of heaven.

19 The core of the nation's life, renewal, survival was only, can only be, and is still for all nations, the moral standard of His law.

20 It was true of Israel when the psalm was written. It is true today of all nations which have known that heritage. Let that truth but be flouted and judgement is still certain.

Read Psalm 148

Occasion and author

Whoever wrote this Creation Hymn was a man who lived vividly in the wonder of the whole universe. Lewis comments perceptively: 'Another result of believing in Creation is to see Nature not as a mere datum but as an achievement. Some of the Psalmists are delighted with its mere solidity and permanence. God has given to His works His own character of *emeth*; they are water-tight, faithful, reliable, not at all vague or phantasmal. "All His works are faithful – He spake and it was done, He commanded and it stood fast" (33.4,9). By His might (Moffatt) "the mountains are made firm and strongly fixed" (65.6). God has laid the foundations of the earth with perfect thoroughness (104.5). He has made everything firm and permanent and imposed boundaries which limit each thing's operation (148.6).'

Commentary

1–14 This is a poem which requires no dissection. Its impact is whole, like J. S. Blackie's hymn which is based on it:

> Sun and moon bright,
> Night and noon-light
> Starry temples azure-floored,
> Cloud and rain, and wild wind's madness,
> Sons of God that shout for gladness,
> Praise ye, praise ye, God the Lord!

Ocean hoary,
Tell His glory;
Cliffs, where tumbling seas have roared,
Pulse of waters, blithely beating,
Wave advancing, wave retreating,
Praise ye, praise ye, God the Lord!

Rock and highland,
Wood and island,
Crag, where eagle's pride hath soared;
Mighty mountains, purple-breasted,
Peaks cloud-cleaving, snowy-crested,
Praise ye, praise ye, God the Lord!

It has been plausibly conjectured that the lines of v. 14 from: 'Praise for all his saints . . .' may be part of an old title to the next psalm which became detached and appended to the earlier hymn. It is not impossible that this is the case and it is clear that the psalm would end more resoundingly with their detachment.

Read Psalm 149; Revelation 5.11–14; Isaiah 60.1–3

Occasion and author

In Neh. 4.17, the Chronicler describes the builders of the wall working with sword in hand. Perhaps this dates the occasion of the psalm. It is a song of victory.

Commentary

1–3 The time-honoured celebration of God's mercies took forms in the Hebrew world which are not necessarily a model for today (Exod. 15.20; Judg. 11.34; 1 Sam. 18.6). C. S. Lewis says a word which the Church might bear in mind. Speaking of the 'gusto' of some of the more joyous psalms, he continues: 'All Christians know something the Jews did not know about what it "cost to redeem their souls". Our life as Christians begins by being baptized into a death; our most joyous festivals begin with, and centre upon, the broken body and the shed blood. There is thus a tragic depth in our worship which Judaism lacked. Our joy has to be the sort of joy which can coexist with that; there is for us a spiritual counterpoint where they had simple melody. But this does not in the least cancel the delighted debt which I, for one, feel that I owe to the most jocund Psalms.'

It is good to rejoice and be glad, but never without reverence, never without awe, never without some touch of the cross.

4,5 'Couches' is odd. Does it mean 'prayer mats' so common in the east (JB and NEB seem to imply this)? Other suggestions are literal. Perhaps it is difficult to realize, for those who have not faced the experience, that it is a joyous thing to go to rest in peace. It is, however, surely not common to 'shout for joy upon one's bed,' as two versions put it.

6-9 It is difficult to imagine the mood of an encircled people, menaced by ruthless foes, not only determined to destroy their place and persons, but to quench a movement of destiny, and obliterate some high purpose of history embedded in a people's way of life. Christian poetry has used similar language to such purpose – Julia Ward Howe's hymn for example, written in Washington when the author and her husband, both ardent for a cause, visited an army camp by the Potomac. It was sung in St. Paul's Cathedral at Winston Churchill's funeral.

> *Mine eyes have seen the glory of the*
> *coming of the Lord:*
> *He is trampling out the vintage*
> *where the grapes of wrath are stored;*
> *He hath loosed the fateful lightning*
> *of His terrible swift sword:*
> *His Truth is marching on.*
>
> *I have seen Him in the watch-fires*
> *of a hundred circling camps;*
> *They have builded Him an altar in*
> *the evening dews and damps;*
> *I have read His righteous sentence*
> *by the dim and flaring lamps:*
> *His Day is marching on.*

Read Psalm 150

Occasion and author

Like the first psalm in the whole Psalter, this concluding doxology was probably the work of the editor of the whole collection.

Commentary

1-6 God is properly praised in His sanctuary but where can the boundary lines of His power, and therefore of His praise be drawn?

His mighty deeds, His sovereign majesty, are the first reason for reverence.

Let every imaginable instrument of worship meet in one mighty orchestra. The hyperbole prepares the mind for the last call . . .

. . . the last call to all Creation to worship God.

Amen and Amen

144